KRISTEN JEWEL

Witches, Queens, & Other Evil Things

KRISTEN JEWEL
WRITING

First edition

ISBN (paperback): 979-8-9921323-4-2
ISBN (hardcover): 979-8-9921323-6-6

Cover art by Kristen Jewel
Editing by Kristen Jewel
Narration by Kristen Jewel
Typesetting by Kristen Jewel

This book was professionally typeset on Reedsy.
Find out more at reedsy.com

For all our witches, queens, and women... who were never really evil things.
(a.k.a.) ~You~

"The whole concept of witches was that women were speaking up for themselves and fighting for their rights. The whole concept of witchcraft came into play to hold down women and women's empowerment."

—Mädchen Amick

***

"I was a princess made of ashes; there is nothing left of me to burn. Now it's time for a queen to rise."

—Theodosia, Ash Princess, Laura Sebastian

***

"Queen, do not allow a commoner to dethrone you. Own that throne. You are royalty."

—Gift Gugu Mona

Contents

Foreword

Kristen and I met through our poetry community on Instagram.

Just the beginning of the book, and I'm sucked in!!! I love how Kristen is so detailed on the layout of the book; she does such an amazing job at picking titles, and they pull you in. The first section is just divine; her words are so powerful and beautiful. The book is so powerful, it stays in your mind! I want to eat her tongue and brain hahaha.

The second section!! This one made me tear up in so many places. Many words cut deep as a woman and as being part of this society and being stuck— it's such a good follow-up to the first part. It's like no matter what, one way or another, we get painted as evil, and it's just impossible to get away from it. I wonder why we are set up this way, why we let ego win over peace.

I loved it; it pulled me in on so many different ways and levels. Made me cry, laugh, and just think—which is one of the best things a book can do, especially poetry, and I love the way it reads. I seriously need her to do an audiobook with this book!

The emotions I go through reading these poems are overwhelming and powerful because they really do spark the right type of rage. The way she breaks down these poems is brilliant. I can see the time she spends on them; each piece is so well-written, the metaphors are amazing, and so are the references! The characters she incorporates, the way she writes their voices, and their misconceptions—it's just fascinating.

Amazing, seriously, so powerful and hitting. It's not calling for violence, but it is awakening the mind. Some things need to be raw and in your face and bitter and evoking. I think this book is so important, and I think she's brilliant. Some pieces are hard, but they are presented in a way that brings them back around to strength.

It's a good balance of accountability, fuck the government, don't twist our feminine rage, and enough realness to make you want to speak, but not cry for days on end.

This book gave me the feeling of resiliency. It's so inclusive and wonderful! Take back our pride and our roots, rewrite the wrong that man-made history has done with our power. I seriously love this!

~Poet Doraly

Preface

Hi, lovely gems.

This book has been in the works for a long time, with poems I've written throughout high school, college, and now.

I want to be clear that feminism is full of intersectionality. While I will not write from the voice of an identity I do not own, I feel it's important to acknowledge the struggles that are different from my own experiences.

The problem with first-wave feminism was that it only wanted to include white, able-bodied, straight, cisgender, rich women—that's not the message I want to send with my book. I recognize that women of color, queer women, trans women, nonbinary folks, and people with disabilities face different, often harsher, experiences and barriers than I can understand from our different lived experiences.

That is to say, don't only listen to my voice on these topics! Definitely check out other poets and writers!! There are so many people speaking about their lived experiences, and we should learn from those outside of ourselves for understanding, but also for empathy; the most powerful thing you can have.

So while this book is a feminist piece, these poems are art created from my lived experiences and the way I perceive the world. And because of the daunting amount of systemic issues we face, I couldn't tackle as many problems as I'd like, but I did my best. I hope that if you read this, you feel empowered and strong <3

Thank you!

Trigger Warnings

The themes of this book tackle some triggering topics: depression, anxiety, self-esteem issues, trauma, violence, assault, abuse, etc. While none of it is overtly graphic, these topics can still be triggering.

If at any time you feel triggered by my words, please stop reading. Your mental health is always top-priority.

If you feel unsafe, please reach out to the 988 Suicide and Crisis Lifeline or your own support systems.

Love always,

Kristen Jewel

Prologue

Don't tell me
you don't
just love
the chaos
I'm brewing.

I

Part One: Witches

What is a witch
but a woman?

.

Siren Song

Sometimes when I sleep,
  I see salt seas swallowing sailors;
  Sirens,
      Summoning
        Singing
          Sinking
            Songs.

Righting all of this world's wrongs.
  .

  .

  .

  What if sirens are reincarnated witches out for revenge?
  Persecuted women, sunk with stones,
  suffering,
  suffocating,
  swallowing sweet-salt sorrow.
  And what are we but drowning in our own salt-tears?

Reincarnated witches' reverse roles in their roles as sirens:
  Drowning sailors with stones of song,

a lament of their own melancholy murder melody.

You know…
    I've never been condemned as an evil witch,
    but I've sure been made to feel like one.

Reincarnated insults rise as endearments—like bitch.
    And in my reincarnation, I wake to salt-sweet brine
    to take whatever vengeance is mine.

I see salt seas swallowing sailors,
    pirates, pillagers, ravagers,

but of drowned witches… somehow…
    All I see are women.
    Not a single one of them
    mythological, fantastical, magical, evil, or even crazed.
    Only innocent women and girls; innocence razed.
    Land grabs, wealth disputes, rejected proposals,
    and suddenly, I understand the sirens;

I see salt seas swallowing sailors, and I, too,
    would love nothing more than to lure murderous men to their salty graves.

To Name Her 'Crazy'

"**W**omen are just SO crazy," the boy quips, spittle flying from his lips.
Like we haven't heard this before.
Hmmmm. Crazy women…

Let's track back—back through time, back through the ages,
    back to ancient gods, civilizations—back to mythology and magic.
    We are in a time of spell-casting and witches, and power; Nomenclature.
    We are in the stories of old, where words come to life.
    To Name a thing… is to hold absolute power over that thing.

And look at *you*, his captive audience—as he weaves his worded spell for you.

The boy is chanting, hands waving,
    his puffed-up chest expels from puffed-up lungs,
    his rib cage can't cage, as he rages: "Women are just SO CRAZY!"

Snaps

And he has us! The spellcaster's words ~transform~ us!

~We turn crazy~

Girls grow into gorgons, snakes swirling where once was hair is no longer there—our glowing glare stones him in place.

Why so petrified? You named us—didn't you?

~We turn crazy~

Bodies twist into gnarled gargoyles, guarding our girls in stone silence.

Are you terrified of us? Horrified by our 'Crazy' defiance?

We become every creature you fear

when we hear how crazy you've Named us.

~We turn crazy~

The word 'crazy' derived as a device devised to undermine women for centuries, memories of 'over-reacting,' 'over-exaggerating,'

he's exacerbating the word as a manipulation

a manifestation of misogyny

calling us 'over-emotional,' 'hysterical,' *CRAZY* women.

Women were murdered, burned at the stake for that shit.

Women were falsely institutionalized for that shit.

Even today, we are losing our rights in this country because of that shit.

~WE TURN CRAZY~

If you want us to be 'crazy,' we can embody insanity animatedly,

transform into banshees, harpies, witches, Valkyries—whatever you please,

but *please*;

Understand: If you Name us 'crazy,'

we get to be as *crazy* as we please.

We Were Witches

We were Witches
We were Wayward
We were Wanton
We were Wicked
We were Wild

We were

We were

We were

We were *Women*.

I Am a Burning Witch

I am a burning witch.

No:

You are not burning me.
—I am not 'being' burned.

It's just that

I am *burning*.

I burn within
I burn without

I am burning with rage and sorrow; fury and doubt

I am a burning witch,
which you cannot burn.

Burned Together

We were burned together,
You and I.
Set ablaze on the pyre,
to bathe in fire and die,
my sister from another life
my soul knew yours before I was alive.
Memory locked away as our bones decayed,
returned to earth and dirt and soil
so our souls could reunite along life's coil
a line so divine
this strand that may never be cut, severed, or untethered.
Fates in three, broken scissors,
ours is the bond that never withers.
Across the great divide,
my life is tied to yours, and yours to mine;
We're the knot, the root, unbreakable
Eternally intertwined.

~For Shelby

Ache

The world is burning
    in a way I can't really comprehend.
      The world keeps turning, but flames lick apart my heart,
slowly charring; hard descend.
There's a soul-deep ache in my chest, a devastated mourn,
an ache I can barely breathe through, terribly forlorn.

Please.
    Take some sandpaper and manually sand this ache from my heart.
    Scrub it down, buff it smooth,
    use whatever toughened methods lead to soothe.
    Prove me malleable, changeable; Transformable.

Prove that even toughened things can make life soft again.
    That even gritty, jaded edges can be smoothed, rounded, polished;
    sharp edges demolished.
    This ache in my heart contains deepened dread, frigid in my stomach,
    feeding my fear that nothing but elbow grease and brute force
    will ever be able to force the ache from my hurt heart.

Spellcasting

If I could cast a spell to make the whole world well,
it would be well worth my burning.
Make no mistake, I would risk that stake
because no good deed goes unpunished.

If I could magic away all the senseless death and violence
I know that they would much prefer my silence.
Any unchecked magic a woman dare to use
only becomes tragic, another woman to abuse.

No interference permitted, only adherence submitted;
submission, suspicious of witches, acquitted,
acquittal, unlikely, a trial unsightly
to burn so brightly; to die by the hand
that you fought for so bravely.

Yet I still wish I could cast that spell
before this whole world
descends into hell.

Indulge Me

P lease

Indulge my wild, witchy, willful ways

Dimensional Seamstress

Bathe me in the waterfall of dreams.
Let the water wash away reality in streams
because reality is never as it seems.
Rushing water cascading through dimensional seams…
Make me a seamstress,
stitching the worlds between waking and dreaming together.
Let the baptismal waters of dream stream around me,
let it flow over me, surround me,
give me hope for all of my tomorrows;
let it wash away my sorrows.

Which Way Witch

Wonder
Which
Way
Witch
Will
Wander

Hopeful Winds

I write hope on the wind, in invisible ink;
 it takes a bit of breath or maybe a flame to reveal this secret.

 I know I share sadness like pie at the holidays,
too sugary and definitely too stuffed, no room for more.

But I wish I shared hope like pollen on a breeze,
 widespread and creating wild blooms.
 Carry like dandelions across yards, implanting in homes
 and creating wishes for those who believe in such superstitions.

I write hope on the wind, not because I don't want it to be seen,
 but because I want it to carry across the world.
 An unseen, unstoppable force only science could explain,
 or maybe even
 just a little magic…

Dandelion Revolution

They say that dandelions are weeds, not flowers;
    A weed that devours grass.

    They say dandelions are toxic,
crowding out that damned green grass in a dandelion invasion;
infestation, a manifestation—
a lawn annihilation.
A dandelion seizure, against our will,
a dandelion commandeer,
a dandelion conquer, if you will.

I'm experiencing an absolute *dandelion thrill.*

Give me dandelion pollution, give me dandelion institution,
    because dandelions might be the solution.

I happen to know that dandelions feed the bees,
    among other things,
    and the bees make honey, and gosh, I love honey.
    It's so funny.

We care more about the plain green grass that feeds absolutely no one
    than we do about a plant we've deemed a menace for no apparent reason
    apart from our own inability to control how it grows.
    Something that actually has a purpose
    and looks pretty too.

So, if society deems you to be a menace
    because it cannot control how you grow
    because you're not a straight-cut, uniform, conforming plain green lawn,
    tries to weed you out, poison you, cut you down, kill you before you've
even begun
    just know, you still have purpose.
    And you look pretty, too.

Because I'd rather be a fine dandelion
    than some patch of grass that never grew.

Withering

Withering hands
    And withering oceans
        Swept with tides, closes and opens
Glaciers and fissures
Cracks are spoken
What are spells but magic broken?
Take a token, have some luck
I'll give you a charm to get unstuck
For prosperity of health
Not of coin or wealth
But body and soul, nature and forest
Leaf and soil, body to body
That's the only toil,
No hidden meanings, no secret malice
Just the joining of body with forest
Soul with earth
Touch our roots
And heal in both.

Mother Earth

Mother Earth is the epitome of resilience.
She gives, we take, and she keeps giving.
Her generosity has never wavered.
We mistreat her, and she still provides.
How kind would it be
if we came together in unity
and showed her how much we want to see her thrive?
Clean the trash that's polluting her beauty.
Treat her lands and oceans right.
Show her we can be better.
Put her first for our own sake.

We trash this planet like we have a second one
    a spare sock in the drawer overflowing with holey ones,
    not holy once,
    bending, breaking, ripping without mending,
    just taking and taking, never-ending.
    Using up all the air
    like we've got a spare tire on the back of a jeep,
    corporations, too cheap to "go green."

We use Mother Earth, like she's replaceable.
  And isn't that just on par with how this planet feels about women?
  A newsflash for nobody, this planet is not replaceable, nor disposable.
  We were supposed to care for her, now despair for her.
  We should have treated her right in the first place,
  grown her flowers, held the door,
  done everything, and more.
  Cared a little more.

When do we realize we can't go back in time?
  There's no fixing all the damage that we caused.
  We can't start fresh; we have to deal with all the problems we created.
  Earth doesn't need us. It will restore itself without us.
  We are nothing if we drain the earth of all its glee.

The enemy is us — is we.
  Because one person can't make a change,
  it takes us all to give back what the earth gives us each day we breathe.
  Learn to love each other and finally let Earth
  be the place where we can all live together in peace.
  Respect and love, just as the earth has shown us, we can be.

We are killing the Earth,
  the only thing that actually nourishes us, nurtures us,
  and haven't we heard not to bite the hand that feeds us?
  The earth needs us, but not as much as we need her.
  We need to do everything we can to save the Earth,
  the trees, the water, the bees, the animals, *please*.
  Please care as much for nature as you do for a dollar.

~Written with Doraly

Cracked Glass and Mirrors

Cracked glass and mirrors,
broken shards litter the floor.
I'm not a seer, but I should have seen this coming.
Should have seen the hit before the gore.
…should have paid attention more.
Haunted pasts and shattered futures,
time is broken, stuck in all my fears.
What are haunted houses compared to the horrors of my mind?
And the scattered mess you left behind.

So, what is illusion if our ghosts only sometimes reappear;
and everything we choose to see… isn't all that is there?
Time is just a collection of our fragments, so when we wake up at the same
time,
but in different time zones,
and we speak mostly the same words, but in different languages.
How related are our journeys?
How intertwined is Poetic Justice?

~Written with Eric

Mithridatism

There are things I don't write about.
      Traumas buried deep
      traumas bubbling to the surface,
the ones that keep me from sleep.
Like a tension-filled water glass.

But there are things I just won't write about.
   There's not a doubt within my soul
   that some things I would write
   would just hurt people.
   It would rip open the wound
   that barely started healing.
   Scabbed over, leftover pus oozing around the edges
   Infected
   Festering
   But I've learned to live with Poison.
   Learned to swallow toxicity.

An emotional form of mithridatism.

Keep swallowing non-lethal doses of poison

until I'm immune to the deaths they cause.

There are things that I just *can't* write about.
  At least, things I can't share.
  Things that would make beautiful art,
  but would destroy my heart in the process.
  And I don't think it's fair that people expect you to share those things.

Like, I *owe* them my trauma.
  Like, what I'm writing is never painful enough,
  never personal enough,
  never rips me open enough.

How entitled of you
  to demand someone else's pain.

How wonderful that it doesn't affect you.
  And I wonder how much pain you swallowed until you grew immune to
it, too.

Blasphemer

A cross dangles between your clavicles;
it *hangs.*

There must be some symbolism in that, maybe a metaphor,
definitely irony.
You preach a story:
say you believe in gods, plagues, and purgatory,
but want to burn the witches and unworthy, barricade the border; won't
feed the hungry.
And I wonder...
With that hanging cross betwixt withered breasts, deceitful breaths,
and fork-tongued lies...
do you fear that crossed metal might be the conduit of your demise?

A direct path for lightning to strike you down
from the pedestal you've pulled yourself up on.
The thing about looking down on people,
placing yourself above,
is that you're now the highest thing attracting lightning to strike.

And be it science or theology,

breaking every commandment or riding your high horse,
both flash warning of being struck where you stand,
so, choose your stance.

Sacrilegious, brazen blasphemer;
be careful of that metal cross worn in hypocrisy over your poisoned heart.
The metal will remain unblemished.

But you?
Made of human flesh and mockery?
Made of hatred, racism, and bigotry?
That cross's conductivity will direct electricity straight from divinity
in baptismal currents of lightning rivers in the name of holy trinity.

Blood for Blood

There's more than one way to kill,
thrill chilling up my spine,
anticipation so divine, like fine wine
as I sharpen forgotten pencils and carve outdated quills,
laying paper like plastic to prepare for how blood spills.

With a hunter's instinct, I ready for the kills.
Lay in wait… draw back blades…
write
until the carcass stills.

It's amazing.
How liars paint truth as persecution—as execution.
Throw accusation of reputation assassination—like I'm the assassin????
Demand restitution,
like, can you even kill me twice?

But if you want to paint me a killer,
I'll gladly become one,
sink down in the mud.
You demand, "Blood for blood."

OKAY.
But,
you'll have to spill a little more blood.
No, wait, a LOT more. Even more,
come on, keep bleeding.
Because we did NOT bleed the same.

Blood for blood?
You led me to the slaughter,
ripped and tore,
bled me dry, covered in my gore,
wore MY heart on YOUR sleeve,
bled me like sacrifice, I bled like a sieve
blood gushing until I had nothing left to give, until I had nothing left to live.

Ravenous vampire, you drank more than your fair share,
more than your fill—you feasted, you gorged on me
so gluttonously.

Fucking please; undead liar.
The truth hurt your reputation? You cried defamation?
Let me show you inflammatory inflammation.
YEAH. Let's do blood for blood,
you'll make me a killer,
a hunter,
you'll make me your assassin
to bleed you half as much as you bled me.

And maybe
when you're empty
you'll finally see:

If the truth hurts your character,
   you were never worthy.
   If the truth hurts your reputation,
   you were never deserving.
   Never had anything worth preserving.
   Even convinced yourself, lying so habitually.

And look.

Now you've made killers of us both
   as I prep the mortuary with notebook paper
   and pen your obituary.

Instagram Spoken

Spoken Version: https://www.instagram.com/reel/DKkpwnuJyUp/?
utm_source=ig_web_copy_link&igsh=NTc4MTIwNjQ2YQ==

Spelling Strawberry

I plucked a strawberry…
picked just the right one;
Perfect size
Perfect shape
Perfect color
Almost resembled…
your tongue…

Set my intentions,
said a prayer,
or was it a chant?
And stabbed it through with toothpicks
one by one.

"Strawberry and rye,
you will not lie,
and if you do,
let loose words be noose,
to hang your tongue by."

I froze that berry raw,

toothpicks and all...
thinking only
to let your own words
be your downfall.

~Dedicated to Ukrainian WitchTok

Thank you!

1

Spoken Version: https://www.instagram.com/reel/DPhCzyQkZ7x/?
utm_source=ig_web_copy_link&igsh=NTc4MTIwNjQ2YQ==

She ATE

I ate your tongue for my dinner—
 Cut into it with the sharpest knife I own.
 It sliced like butter.
Did the home of your hatred always cut so easily?

I ate your tongue for my dinner—
 Sprinkled pepper across your salt-packed taste buds,
 were your words always this over-salted?
 I'm no chef or doctor, but even I know too much sodium can kill.

I ate your tongue for my dinner—
 Snatched the words right out of your mouth,
 a word feast I swallowed whole.
 Chewed the spongy bits until they were palatable;
 your delivery always did need work.

I ate your tongue for my dinner—
 and man, your tongue-lashing sure tastes different.
 Tastes almost bitter. Sharp. Exacting.
 Have you ever tasted your own words?
 Ever bit your own tongue?

Dug your teeth in so harshly, copper blood would flood your mouth?
You really should have.
But since you didn't bite your tongue, I'll bite it for you.

I'll eat your tongue for my dinner—
    bite and chew until your words
    soften enough to really digest.

What's that you say?
    You say that's sick? Repulsive, disgusting, and morbid?

You're right. I agree.

Eating your tongue for my dinner was absolutely appalling.
    Gag-inducing, rife bile;

I've never tasted such *vile* in my life.

Girl Death

P ause girl dinner,
    give me girl death.
      I do not want to die in a fiery blaze of fury and glory,
flames melting flesh from skin,
blood boiling from within, cauterizing clothes to bones.

I think enough of my matriarchy has burned to death at the stake.

For the sake of pain, I want a gentle death.
    Painless.
    A death of peace and comfort.
    Be it poison in my tea
    or slipping away in my sleep so quietly.

I do not care about the perception of my death.
    I do not care how cool it would look to die in a war nobody even wanted.
    I don't care if my death looks like the baddest shootout and bleed out.
    I don't care how the end of my life looks to those still alive.
    But I sure as fuck care how it feels.
    I do not want fear, suffering, and agony;
    I do not want prolonged torture

my life itself gave me all the suffering I could handle.

I want peace in my death.
  I want it warm and cozy and gentle.
  With the softest blankets and no bra.
  I barely want to feel it.
  Like being lulled to sleep,
  or smoothly floating over ocean waves,
  rocking me softly away.

Yeah. I definitely want girl death.

No Magic

I'm not groundbreaking;
   not earth-shaking, nor shattering,
   I'm just taking each word, syllable by syllable
until I'm able to make sense of absurd.

To process feelings: sad and mad and glad,
   to understand myself until peace can be had.
   I'm not moving mountains or walking on water
   no miracles or magic fountains, no sacrifices or slaughter.
   I have nothing new or shocking, no innovating.
   I'm sorry these words are so lackluster,
   not enough, not nearly, not awe-appealing, just stuff I'm feeling.

I understand that I am not good enough; funnily enough,
   I have never *been* enough—enough of this.
   I might be lacking to the masses, but I've never been for them.
   Don't hold too much for unproductive criticism;
   I have too much of my own cynicism,
   the prison of expectation as tight as a cage,
   can't perform the extraordinary if you're locked away.

Spit Fire

Sometimes,
I want to spit fire.

Maybe literally and metaphorically,
use enough rhymes and bars to set off alarms,
get the whole fucking fire department involved.

Sometimes I think my words are not enough.
Not the ones I speak,
and certainly not the ones I don't let leak.
The ones I confine, keep back, hold tight.

I think if I said what was on my mind,
I could burn down entire cities.

…Or regimes…

Barren Ground

S ometimes, my heart feels bereft.
     A battleground left scarred and charred,
     scorching earth so hard; nothing can grow anymore.
Trauma has left the soil burnt and infertile.
Nothing can bloom here.
The root-deep veins flowing from my body cut short at the heart.
Like a chopped-down tree,
roots unearthed, hacked separately.
And if my heart is a felled tree,
I'd beg you to just leave it be.
You've already ripped it from the earth;
do not salt the ashes to prevent rebirth.
Let them enrich the surrounding soil,
let something new be born from the ashes.
If there's anything I've learned from phoenixes, forest fires, and controlled
burning,
     it's that even growth is possible in barren ground.

My Poetry is Necromancy

My poetry is necromancy;
    Raising the Dead from long-buried, soil-packed graves.
    And if fury were a graveyard,
I would raise
every
body
in it.
Dead things crawling free from churned earth,
nails packed with dirt, clawing their way to the surface.

My rage boils over into the land of the dead.
    And when I step into that decaying plane of existence, I see this world;
    Crumbling.
    And yet, I see no difference.

I see history repeating itself across the globe—Ukraine, Gaza, Congo, Sudan,
the United States, and *more*.
    I see genocide and hatred, children dead, denied food and medical aid.
    It wasn't even the bombs that killed them;
    it was us.
    Our inaction, and our actions to prevent help.

Our further actions to help the wrong side.

So many people lost their lives so senselessly; more than a tragedy, it's a travesty.

This devastation is... indescribable. Unforgivable.

ICE, kidnapping people in the streets, from schools, from homes,
  'maga' cheering the atrocity
  with the audacity befitting a fucking Nazi.

My poetry is necromancy.

I am the necromancer,
  compelled to raise the dead
  with my dead-speech.
  But...
  I bite my tongue.
  Kill my words.
  This resurrection is for fury;
  not bodies.
  Bodies at rest should stay at rest.

I step back into the plane of the living and still see our crumbling world...
  And I don't care how many apathetic, living-dormant-tombstones I have to touch
  to bring life to outrage, and not just for the dead;
  outrage for what we *keep allowing* to happen to our living.

My poetry is necromancy.
  The most Evil of magics.

And I hope it keeps us rolling in our graves of apathy.

2

II

Part Two: Queens

While Witches Are Wicked
And Dragons Are Dreadful
Evil Queens Are SO Quintessential
And All

~Breathe Fire~

I Dream of Queendom

I dream of Queendom

Not for a kingdom.

I dream of Queendom

Not to command anyone to bow,

But so I may never be commanded to bow to anyone.

Empire Dreams

I dream of Empires
 Not for waistlines
 but to waste 'Lines.'
No more eugenics. No more family 'Names.'
No more make-believe 'perfect genes'—OR jeans.

I dream of Empires under matriarchies.
 Not for the sake of power or control,
 but to enforce the care of ALL people.
 Empires of care, of love, of radical acceptance.

I dream of Empires that protect the people's existence.
 Not personified corporations or unethical billionaires
 but real, everyday people.

Yeah, I dream of Empires,
 not kingdoms on hilltops closed off by tall spires,
 but Queendoms in open fields that nurture and inspire.

No Kings

Empty screams
Bitter lies
Empty hearts
Shitty lives
Evil kings
Take innocent lives
While 'Evil Queens'
Get shamed and blamed,
Villainized, despised, and demonized.
I think it's time…
To sharpen knives.

Mother, Maiden, Crone

Mother, Maiden, Crone,
   I think I've grown into my own.
      Fuck the pedestal, I stole the throne; crown the witch, make her a queen, and she'll show you power unseen.

But where they hold torches and pyres, she holds compassion and flowers.
   She'll hold your hand, she'll heal your soul,
   even though you've been nothing but awful.
   You glare at her with disdain, spit at her in distaste,
   but boy, you're the only one showing disgrace.

I've never seen anything more "Christ-like"
   than a witch turning the other cheek.
   She doesn't curse your bloodline, but by the goddess, I wish she would.
   She recognizes that innocent children do not hold the sins of their parents.

Mother, Maiden, Crone,
   I really have grown into my own.
   While society decries, "Witch!" at every nonconforming woman,
   I see a Queen embracing herself fully, finally, coming into her own
   with abandon, a royal finale.

Stay Golden

Bathe me in liquid gold
    until I embody wicked, bold.
    I wish I had audacity, beauty, ferocity
I want to saunter and sway, I want to lift my chin confidently.

So, let me bathe in liquid gold until I embody royalty.
    Shed my skin like a snake, exfoliate with each golden flake,
    inspire loyalty, I crave to be met with fealty
    when I'm coated in golden skin.
    Can I scrub my skin gone?
    Melt my flesh away? Replace it until the skin I wear is shiny?

I'll wear gold like armor,
    head held high, like nothing can touch me.
    And if, in turn, everything I touch turns to gold,
    I hope you let me hold your heart, since it's already golden.
    There's no danger of stopping it cold, and
    I'll protect it with these armored hands,
    keeping your heart's purity.
    We're untouchable, confident, saucy, emboldened, frozen;
    We both stay golden.

Caffeine and Hatred

I'm a goddess, I'm a queen,
the best at my behest,
the loveliest sight
your pretty eyes have ever seen,
will ever see,
don't make a scene.
I'm not the prettiest,
but I might be the pettiest,
because to be the best—
I don't need beauty,
I don't need diamonds,
no cheat sheets or technicalities,
just hatred and caffeine.

~For Mother Duck, Amorette

Bleeding Succeeding

I wonder if I need your hate to make something of myself.
   Because I have never been more successful
   than when I'm put down
let down
down and out
outcast
predicted last.
You said you **hate** it when I win,
and *boy*,
I've never stacked my shelves
with more trophies in my *life*,
winning, in spite of strife.
The best revenge I have
is succeeding where you left me bleeding.

~I have left my name in places that will haunt you for centuries~

It's the least I could do to repay you for the blood-soaked finger memories.

Rolling Heads

You once told me:
"Never hang your head for anyone."

Then proceeded
To do everything in your power to hang mine.

Too bad for you
Queens have been fighting to hold on to their heads for centuries.

And Evil Queens?
They'll chop your fucking head off.

So, go ahead; you try that rope. But I promise you now,
Thine rolls before mine.

Paint the Roses

If my head is going to roll,
      you'd better cut it off clean.
      Don't leave a gap, a thread,
or any loose end,
only the sharpest axe for a queen.
Paint my roses red with the blood of my head, and
I'll join your garden of bodies
of all the women you've beheaded.
A garden graveyard—gritty, grave, and grim.
A preview of where you're headed, too,
a cemetery planted with your sin.

Rhyme Queen

The Queen of Hearts, she loved her tarts
The knave stole them away
Off with his head; that man is now dead
And now we play croquet
They called her evil in their fear
But don't you know
We're all mad here?

The White Witch of Narnia
ruled a land so lost
without their golden lion there
She covered it with frost

Maleficent, queen of all things dark
A dragon in true form
Slip the spindle, a needle, pricking, sharp
She really left her mark

Queen Narissa from *Enchanted* was a dragon, too
Never threaten her rule
Or dragon's fire is for you

Anointed Evil

We have so many infamous evil queens portrayed in books, TV, and movies—
      I can name ten from the tip of my tongue;
we have so many to choose from.
    But tell me, of evil kings… from the tip of your head, can you name me one?

How is it we see so many faces when we say "Evil Queen"—the term anointed—
    but 'Evil King'
    sounds so terribly disjointed.
    We stretch our minds like book spines
    to come up with one in fiction when nonfiction is overflowing with them.

—What is this addiction to propaganda, picture-perfect patriarchy?
    and the message of miserably murderous, malicious matriarchy?

Evil Queens

I have a predilection for Evil Queens.
Evil Queens, and all their vengeant schemes.

In *Snow White*, the Evil Queen poisoned a child because her mirror was beguiled, saying she was pretty—how petty, but we all know bad apples.

And when they called Ursula a witch, you KNOW what they really meant was "bitch."
Sea, bitch; she was the one who REALLY ruled the seven seas.

Cersei Lannister burned her enemies alive with wildfire, and now she's the one they're all calling sire.
She'll sip her wine and be just fine in the gaudiest attire.

It's funny how women in power are often portrayed oh so very, very sour.
Because they are not princesses, helpless in a tower, they cower for no one.

Snow White's Queen is so relatable, as beauty is *demanded* of us—it's a shame not many know her name despite her fame—but I guess that's the price of pretty—pretty inane
Since some say she was inspired by the Countess Báthory,

a woman propagandized to have bathed in virgin's blood to stay beautiful, youthful,

and yet we claim virginity isn't a social construct?

Sexual conduct 'obviously' detracts from beauty—

And we all know a queen's 'wifely duty' — how could she not be embarrassed?

It makes me wonder if Snow White was dubbed the fairest in the land, not for her face,

but because man's hand will soil you.

Was she the fairest for how 'unspoiled' her body was?

Disgusting.

Somehow, a dick makes you impure; slandered,

how can anyone adhere to this societal standard?

We've pandered to the conceited notion that a flesh-stick could change someone at all.

Maybe THAT was the queen's downfall.

Maybe we should have offered apples to mirrors telling us we are flowers;

Once plucked, we die—that's what it means to be fucked.

Just *try* to judge my beauty or 'purity'

when you're choking on the vengeance I feed—

"—You poor, unfortunate souls."

Power does not make witches of us.

Ursula knew that, and she knew what she was about; no doubt that empowerment was why she was cast out in the first place, no place for confident queens—not only comfortable—but *seductive* in their skin.

To them, could there be any worse sin?

They tried to stereotype female power, queerness, and fat as 'evil'

but it backfired—she's an icon, iconic, with her voluptuous curves—

—the people KNOW the Sea Queen SERVES with her hip-swish-sway-sashay.

Have we ever seen a more devious diva?!

They had to banish her for her audacity.

And you know, I would charge for souls too, if they tried to destroy mine with such tenacity.

You want to strip me naked for a walk of atonement? Because I can only atone through the mercies of gods unknown,

for sins judged by men to be indecent?

I will walk your righteous path, feet bleeding on the stones, but never forget this is a *game of thrones*.

And there is no purer way to atone than bone going up in flame and smoke.

Cersei will burn her enemies where they stand because she is the baddest bitch in that western land.

Call her the mad queen if you will, but she knows there is more than one way to kill, she slays—

so SLAY, QUEEN, SLAYYY!

We are so afraid of women's power.

So, try to keep us locked in a tower—trapped, beaten, assaulted, and murdered—while policy refuses to change,

the only change they fight for is to take even more of our rights away.

So many women are dying from domestic violence—but assure us, "It's not all men."

And yet, guys like brock turner only serve three months locked up, which is a miracle when most rapists never see a day in jail, yet they keep drilling into us: "Not all rapists are male."

Somehow, kneeling for a song was judged a greater societal wrong than knocking a woman out in an elevator; it's an indicator of how important they think women are.

They'll burn a jersey, saying peaceful protest is a greater controversy than assault and abuse.

I guess it's no use

to beg them to stop killing us.

Do not come crying to us when we embrace the destructiveness implanted in our bodies through violence; you've been far too comfortable sitting in silence.

I have a predilection for Evil Queens,
    I love their fury, their malice, retribution, so callous.
    And you may call us evil queens, because we have been shown EXACTLY what evil truly means.

So, forgive me if I'd rather be a *queen* than a *peasant*
    and I'd rather be *NASTY* than pleasant.

And to those who refuse to see our plight,
    or perpetuate it from their unholy chapel,
    I have a question:

How would you like a bite...
    of a shiny red apple?
    3

Apple

Apple...

Temptation fruit.

What went through her mind, I wonder...

Imagine-it-was-me

where

snakes of men lie to lay,
  prey upon your insecurities to get their way,
  make you fall to their level,
  plucking you off the branch of your morals and biting into your core.
  They devour your resistance, and whatever is left wishes to please the unappeasable,
  until you finally do the most degrading thing to make them happy—

Take a bite.

But remember: *You're* the Evil Thing in this tale.

Apple Preaching

The man shouts: "Women are original sin!"

Every time she seeks education.
Every time she seeks validation.
Every time she seeks a vacation
from home labor or even appreciation.

It's started to make me think...
maybe he just hates women.

How can my entire existence be damned just by existing?
I didn't ask to be here, certainly wouldn't choose to.

The church made me lose faith in the church.
Not the devil, not a snake, not a demon—
not the temptation they preached would reach me.
It was just simple men and women preaching sermons of hatred,
who made me hate myself,
made me sorry I ever existed.

But this is the story of how I've resisted.

Dear church,

    The way you speak about women

    makes me want to never step foot into a church again.

    In fact, I'd rather burn in hell for eternity

    than listen to another degrading sermon.

    I saw you turn away a desperate woman

    begging for formula; you won't even feed a starving baby, helpless, in need,

    crying out, the greatest vulnerability.

    Pro-life? Right.

    You failed the social experiment with your unholy mentality.

    I'd rather spend my life helping the people around me, loving them unconditionally—but sure, the sinner here is *me*.

Maybe Eve felt the same,

    because if you tell someone over and over

    that they will fail before they've even begun,

    you'll drive them to choose to fall,

    after all,

    she bit dusk's apple, and the knowledge sung.

    If you tell me I'm a sinner just by being here,

    a place I never wanted to be,

    I'll adorn that thorn crown myself,

    and see just how much "sin" is really in me.

I will love others radically, unconditionally, with empathy

    and if that's a sin,

    I'll burn forever so fucking comfortably.

"A Few Bad Apples"

If
there's a drop of poison in
the apple barrel, I bet you won't eat
them at all. Toss the toxic out, go to the tree,
pluck anew. Say a prayer, sign of the cross,
bless fresh fruit, say, "Amen." But just
remember, it's not all...

...apples...

Apple Picking

Take me to the orchard,
   let me walk the rows of trees,
   breathe the air, feel the breeze.
You can smell the season of fall,
and apples are best plucked right after the first freeze,
first frost,
right before all the leaves are lost.
Take me apple picking,
let me pick my most ripe finds
before they rot away, fermented, like nature's wines.
Kill the fruit. Take a bite, drink the juice.
Like a queen before the poison,
not a killer,
just a woman
cast in golden light, enjoying apples, gazing at a setting horizon.

Emerald Seems

I don't associate green with a lot of positive things.
Green is envy,
green is money.
Green is grass (which I still need to touch).
I just don't find much positive emotion linked to green.

So imagine my disappointment when my birthstone turned out to be a shade
of green.
Born in May,
Emerald is my shade.

Oh, maybe that's the trick—"shades."
To look at it in a different way,
a different shade,
a different hue,
a different point of view.

Emerald doesn't have to be straight-up green.
They're in the same family, but they look completely different.
They mix completely different.
They act completely different.

So, that's how I've come to love the word Emerald.
  The word sounds regal.
  I've come to love the shade of Emerald,
  a precious Jewel fit for a queen,
  a darker shade of green,
  that must mean something.

Maybe I'm just made for gemstone shades.
  And I don't mean by royalty, I mean by deeper colors.
  More depth.
  I mean, same tree, but different fruits falling from barren branches.
  And maybe this metaphor is a little too deep,
  but that's how I like my greens.
  Too deep,
  rich in color,
  just like Emerald seems.

Love in Green

I never knew I loved green
  till you grew a garden from your thumb.
  You've tasted death, thought you were numb,
ready to die when your life had barely begun.
Tasted gunmetal gray, trying to chase dark thoughts away
but stayed that finger on that trigger—you Stayed. You Stay.
And I know you only see death and decay in your body, your being,
but girl, how are you not seeing?

Your body gives life.
  You sprouted flowers in the barren, a triple threat,
  thrice life you gave, twice lives you saved, and one heart you've grown.
  You've shown you bear life so gracefully, and I adore you so gratefully,
  grateful me, and lovely you
  borne from primordial ooze.
  I've written your love a million times,
  but I could never write enough; you've given more lives.

You grow a garden in your home,
  keep plants alive I'd kill in a week, but have the nerve to think you're weak?

You, creator of life and love,
    got me thinking god is a woman above.
    Growing life with that green thumb, green body, green being,
    you are an emerald dream filled with serenity, my Green Queen.

I never knew I loved green,
    but girl, body, spirit, soul;
    you are the most beautiful,
    the loveliest, most gorgeous, stunning shade of green
    my poor eyes will ever be blessed to have seen.

Weaving Ivy Crowns

Ivy creeps by limb and vine
   in the dark where leaf and moon intertwine.
   It grows, it climbs, spiral and wind,
and wind, and wind, around and around.
Ivy is so pretty…
until deadly weight overtakes the tree.
Such a pretty, deadly thing.
Intricate swirls and patterns,
looking delicate and divine, until vine breaches brick;
demolishing house and building in kind.
Call me royally mad, call me twisted, as I weave stem and vine together by hand.
For what have I to fear of deadly, heavy plants? Or crushing weight?
When what's in my mind is already crushing, cracking, consuming, shattering, so unbearably heavy and unkind.
I'll weave a perfect circle to join and bind, place atop my hair,
in mock coronation to crown the Queen of Madness
as Ivy crowns the broken mind.

Instagram Spoken

Spoken Version: https://www.instagram.com/reel/DQQlPDjDj3X/

69

The World is Mad, but I'm Madder

The state of the world is mad,
    but I've honed anger like a skill,
    honed insanity like swordplay,
a blade made to kill.

I've trained in darkness, survived,
   somehow, still alive.
   I did not claw my way out of the depths of hell
   to let jokers clown around,
   riding too-small bikes, chiming with a ding and a bell,
   juggling my rights,
   honking red noses,
   slapstick comedy,
   like we're the laughingstock,
   like it's a party trick,
   and not a chopping block.

I've already fought my war,
   lost battles,
   wounded, scarred, torn,
   but still here.

Still standing.
Spine straight like a queen falsely facing a guillotine.
Only, I kept my head,
so, what makes you think you can break my spine now?

The state of the world is mad,
   but I've sharpened fury like a machete.

Go ahead, try to break my spine, snap it, crack it up, and you'll see
   just how much madness lives in me,
   how terribly petty I can be.
   Because if you manage to kill me,
   the hell with you,
   I'll drag you to hell with me—
   We'll see if you still think it's funny burning for eternity.

Princess

I'm not sure why anyone would
want to be a princess
locked in a tower
Taught to cower
taught to curtsy
taught courtesy
above safety.

Drilled politeness
drilled kindness
drilled meekness
drilled weakness
drilled that his ego
is more important
than your comfort,
more important than
your bodily autonomy.

Drilled silence;
drilled to die quietly, alone.
Drilled to hide tears

in bloodstained hands
Die quietly, princess,
die politely for the man.
Literally, fuck the patriarchy.
Fuck any man who thinks
he has the right to take a life.

The violence in this world is mad,
but it's nothing next to our anger.
Fuck being a princess in a tower,
we're so tired of watching
girls and women and people die;
of feeling like we have no power.

4

Queen of the Underworld

They say I'm simple,
    that I'm dumb.
        Light and airheaded,
brain full of pollen;
I spoke with flowers,
so my mind must be numb.

What they don't know
  is that blossoms can thrive in death.
  And even I,
  embodiment of growth and life,
  can see the beauty in death's bloom
  the sanctity of Death's fruit.

Stolen away?
  Me?
  You really think so?

As if I don't feel peace in the land of the dead,
  like it doesn't resonate with my Kore.
  As if I wasn't the one who demanded to stay,

who tasted succulent pomegranates,
licking away wine stains from steady fingertips.

Think I'm an airhead all you wish,
as I'm posted up on my throne,
kicked back, heels high—hell overthrown.
I took over so fast, your head whirled.
But sure, *I'm* the stupid one:
Now bow down to your new Queen of the Underworld.

Nothing Queen

I am the queen of nothing
    The void in space and time
    Black holes and pocket dimensions,
the in-between, unseen, the read between the lines rhymes.
I soothe crystal worry stones betwixt shaking hands,
sip citrus bergamot tea.

I want to speak the names of the dead,
    but I do not want to profit from their deaths.
    I try to kill compulsive fingers, twisting already split-end, deadened hair.
    But there's something about the feeling
    of snapping between my fingers that's terribly satisfying.
    I have trouble leaving the dead alone.
    But I am the queen of nothing and no one
    Nobody.
    Have no voice for the living nor the dead.

It feels like I can't do anything for anyone, myself included, with fingertips
tangled in hair,
    so why do I even exist?
    Am I meant for backgrounds and fade-to-black cut scenes?

Am I the master of making myself small? Invisible?
There is something in me that's asleep.
Something terrible and dark,
something I think is waking despite efforts to keep it dormant.

What radicalized our crystal-loving,
   tea-drinking,
   anxious, hair-twisting woman?
   The better question is... what didn't radicalize me?
   I am the queen of nothing
   So, I guess...
   I have nothing... which is my everything to lose.

Mastering Misery

I'm Miss Mad Monarchy,
  mastering misery;
  making my mind's morbid masterpiece.
My muses, muted; morosely mutilated, musty, mutated... mangled.

Muddy, moldy, malformed mildew morsels
  make my malady-murals more multifaceted.

Murals mirroring mythical, mystical, murderous, mesmerizing mermaid melodies.
  My moping mind... made mischievous...

Make my mural-memorial... masquerade—masking murky misery.

Make my memory... macabre,
  my memoriam... musing moon-sick memoirs, moonstruck melodies, moon-flower mourning,
  maybe maroon marigolds,
  mayhap mulled mulberry.

Memorialized, miraculous, magic.

Majestic?
More maddening...
maybe misunderstood...
me...
Miss Miserably Miserable.

Move, Misery
  —mere misty mirage mythology;
  Minds must murderously mute myth.
  My misery-mutiny manifested,
  moreover, materialized,
  meaningful, messy, magnificent masterpieces.

This... is Misery Mastery.

Villain Arc

I want to write about becoming evil,
roil in my villain arc and era,
embrace my royal evil queen.
But the truth is…
I'm really just tired of people being mean.
I'm tired of people pretending to be friends
while every 'joke' is at someone's expense, plain bullying.

I'm tired of men thinking I am stupid or incapable.
I'm tired of the insufferable.
Tired of people without empathy.
I'm tired of the government and every politician making it their life's
mission to ruin women's lives, livelihoods, and happiness.
Stripping our rights, mocking our fights,
like it's funny to want to be treated as human.

I want to write about my villain arc,
like I'm empowered and strong.
Like my feminist anthem,
my feminine rage song.
But really, my soul is so fucking tired.

My body is fighting me,
    and I can't even have bodily autonomy.
    There's so much injustice around me, surrounding me,
    and I just feel <u>stuck</u>.
    Hopeful but hopeless dichotomy.
    Feeling like I really can't do anything,
    and that doesn't sound like an evil queen.
    That just sounds like women suffering.

I heard a poem from Ayanna Gay— "Busy Body"
    and she said she still has to do the laundry—and isn't that our stark truth?
    We're trapped in a quandary.
    How can we be expected to go about our lives like normal
    while in the middle of a fucking genocide?
    In the middle of government shutdowns and starving the poor?

I want to rage, embrace evil, quit my job, and help people.
    But I'm too poor to quit, body too broken to rage,
    and that's how you know the system has won—they've trapped us.
    I crave to be in my villain era; in reality, I'm just a zoo animal locked in a
cage.

III

Other Evil Things

If anything is evil, it's not women: it's everything society kills us with.

Beautifully Evil

You know what's really evil?
(Unobtainable) societal beauty standards—standards like the norm, like an expectation.
We must obtain the unobtainable through suffering—painful surgeries, diets, and self-harm.
And if we can't?
Well then, we must be evil.

Back to Beauty

Of all the things I write,

I keep coming back to beauty;

How ugly.

Ugly

I think it's entirely human to struggle with feeling ugly.
With being ugly.
I've found my face too round, my chin too double,
let me break it down by the pound, even if this gets me in trouble.
I hate my face, I hate my arms,
I hate my stomach,
I could endlessly list my lack of charms
even if it harms not only me,
but everyone around me.
The hate train keeps chugging,
and I keep juggling all my hate like bowling pins.
Hop aboard and hate today,
because hey,
you couldn't possibly hate me
any more than I hate myself, anyway.
You think mean words can hurt me,
but honey, I promise,
you haven't said anything about me originally.
You've never said anything about me
I don't already tell myself organically.

The Three Bears Would NEVER

First, I was too small,
　　and now,
　　I'm too big.
I have never been the perfect size.
But I just want to say:

I'm not a fucking bowl of porridge.

I am not made for your consumption,
　　something to devour
　　until you find me "just right."

You are not Goldilocks,
　　just an asshole,
　　and you're making me choose the bears.

Unbearable

You know, for someone who sees the worst in everyone,
you don't seem to see me.
And I don't mean you don't see the worst in me,
I mean, you really don't see me.
Like I'm invisible.
Visible enough to criticize.
Hair not long enough, too long, not blonde enough,
but I wonder if you ever see beyond physical appearance.
Or imperfect appearances.
I have to say, calling everyone you see ugly
high-key makes you look ugly. Inside and out.
Cuz I'd rather look unfashionable
than let my personality be unbearable.
How ugly a legacy you leave.
No one will speak of your beauty, the fleeting physical,
but they sure will talk about your actions, words,
and how you made people feel.
And you make me feel invisible.

Beastly Beautiful

Girl: There is a beast that gnaws our bellies and draws long our face,
Tells us we aren't good enough—[**we can't exist in this space.**]

Beast: —[**You can't exist in this space.**]
Face it, darling. You're only worth your face. Beauty is skin deep, and you'll never be as beautiful as—

Girl: —the beast. She's beautiful. So thin, ripe with conceit and scorn, confidence and poise, her voice; heaven. Your will, her toy. She mangles your mind with morbid maybes. Maybe I'd be better off... maybe if I shed it off... maybe if I cut it off; maybe I'd be worth more if there was less.
Less feeling, less clothing, less to think about, think without a thought as to how much she enjoys this...

Beast: I'm ecstatic. Elated in ecstasy, the pleasure erotica I reap in your torment, ferment your thoughts until you're rotten to the core—at least you'll be skinny then. Society says skinny is sexy, smooth skin seductive; cellulite, sickening.

Girl: Your mother always said, "Be emboldened by your beauty." But since you've moved out, your perceptions grew.
Of course, there are others...

Girl: [More fair than you. More fit than you. More alive than you.]

Beast: [More fair than you. More fit than you. More alive than you.]

Look what she has. You'll never have hips like her; You'll never have lips like her. You'll never measure up, and what are you, an A-cup? Just look at her eyes and despise everything you are; look how far you've fallen.

Girl: It's a siren's song, calling you to the depths of yourself; drowning out your voice, make not a noise, be grateful. Gratefully drown in your inadequacy, don't beg, can't be borrowed, tomorrow you'll take a breath only to realize how far she's taken you.

Beast: Drown with me. I'll take you down with me. Frown with me, until I'm all you see, until I'm all you'll be, I'm the beast that won't let you free.

Girl: As you drown in her womb, another beast is born, with the same scorn reflecting in your eyes: one with gleaming red [Talons]

Beast: [Talons] sharpened for the kill.

Girl: War-painted, made-up [Makeup]

Beast: [Makeup] to hide the truth.

Girl: There is no hope for you now... as you sneer at the girl you just called a cow.

Beast: My battle is won. My disease has spread, another victim successfull y dead. I am the malicious, fictitious voice of society, edging you closer to the knife. Carve out your imperfections [Bit By Bit]

Girl: [Bit By Bit] but they won't be

satisfied by any of it.

Girl: [It's pointless. Useless.]

Beast: [It's pointless. Useless.]
But try, darling.

Try to look any way

other than the way

you do.

5

~Written with my primordial ooze twin, Shelby Love

Girl: Written by Shelby

Beast: Written by Kristen

Wear Out Beautiful

I want you to wear out the word "Beautiful."

Like: Soles to shoes
Like: Holes to jeans
Like: Pens to poems
Like:

I want you to wear out beautiful, so I have no doubt how you feel about my soul
Because there's more than one type of beautiful.

I want you to wear out beautiful until my ears are numb and I roll my eyes,
Saying,
"You always say that."

I want you to wear out beautiful until it doesn't mean anything anymore.

So when you don't even think to think about saying it…
It won't mean anything anymore.

See, society got me so fucked up; the only value I see in me is beauty.

Say:

I'm Beautifully inspirational

Beautifully sensational

Beautifully relatable

Beautifully intelligent

Beautifully eloquent

Let's wear out worn-out "beautiful"

Until the word standing on its own is:
  Unsuitable
  Unusable
  Refutable
  Beautifully:

        Removable.

Dressed-Up Evil

S peaking of true evil,
in the same breath they demand impossible beauty,
they decry our bodies, skin, and clothes.
Use clothes to control, act as permission for violation.

Leggings Are My Only Pants Now

"Giiiirl—leggings are *not* pants," he sniffs, nose in the air, and it's clear where his glare is directed.

Eyes glued to her ass like cement to the ground, his gaze indicates that he doth protest too much.

See, when his balls finally dropped, he started thinking with his cock rather than his thoughts; what made *hard*—worse than soft.

So now he feels vindication to dictate how she *should* and *shouldn't d*ress.

Because, as a 'man', he feels entitled to define the definition and description for decency:

"Skirts should be short so I see some skin, smoothly soft and shaven; but not too short, or I'll say you're a slut. Shirts showing a bit of tit are required; anything more and you're a whore, anything less and you're a prude. Please wear short-shorts, don't wear fishnets, there's a difference between classy and trashy, 'I want a lady in the streets but a freak in the sheets'—LEGGINGS ARE NOT PANTS—"

AHHHHH—

You make me want to run to the store and buy EVERY single pair of leggings off that shelf.

I will wear them loud and proud and laugh at the disapproval on your disapproving face.

Don't like what you're clearly ogling? Then stop boring your eyeballs into my body like a dick.

You like *too much* what you're glaring at?

Then stop gawking at my figure and get your shit figured out.

I wear what I do for me—not you

and if you can't handle that?

Go fuck yourself, cuz I'm not doing it for you.

I will parade around wearing nothing but bare skin and judgment until you *know* what indecency looks like.

I will strut my stuff back and forth

forth and back,

upside-down and sideways,

embracing MY body the way I should be free to.

Don't you *dare* judge her before you even know her *name*.

You can't judge her self-worth… by legging.

Vultures

"That outfit leaves nothing to the imagination—"
Stop.
Stop imagining me
In fact,
Stop perceiving me
Let me exist
Invisibly
Stop making me look over my shoulder paranoidly,
Every time I leave the house
Paralyzing paranoia,
I could peel my skin off.
Like oranges.
But those are still consumed... aren't they?
By the ravenous,
Slurping juices,
Like vultures,
Are you circling
Just waiting to devour who falls first?
Whoever looks consumable
Or at least
Like they wouldn't fight back?

I dream of existing
In a world
Free from your imagination
Because I fear,
It's not only unimaginative,
But also chalk-full
Of carnage.

Spoken Version: https://www.instagram.com/p/DPtOo5UDoB2/? utm_source=ig_web_copy_link&igsh=NTc4MTIwNjQ2YQ==

Instagram Spoken

Open Letter to a Shitty DJ

This is an open letter to the boy who lifted my skirt up in the middle
of a bar,

I'll say to you now what I said to you then:
Who the fuck do you think you are?

Oh—I know—you think you're entitled to me, my body, see
you asked me if I wanted to *"fight* about it outside,"
as if you were in the right.

Heart pounding, mind racing, it wasn't *my* life that flashed before my eyes;
it was every woman who has ever been scared into silence,
threatened with violence, forced into compliance.

Everything deep within me rose in defiance.
You, *boy,* do not understand how many scenarios flashed before my eyes.
Inside, I raged, I seethed—outraged—
For every woman who *couldn't* stand up for themselves,
for every woman who has *died* standing up for herself,
for every woman too afraid of confrontation, too scared to get help.

So I said, *"yes,"* for *myself* and for *them*—
    I wanted to fucking "fight about it outside."

You only stepped aside when another guy stepped between us,
    stepped in before it got worse,
    but it did get worse when the man who stepped between us said it, "wasn't
that big of a deal—*it's just a skirt.*"

But it was a big deal to *me*.
    I have the *right* to my body autonomy.

You tried to apologize, like I owed you my forgiveness.
    Like I owed your pittance of an apology acceptance—except I don't—owe
you OR forgive you OR accept this.
    You are not entitled to my forgiveness just because you demand it,
    command it,
    hand it off to me to purge your guilt by accepting your sorry apology.

You stalked me around that bar for far too long after I told you to leave me
alone, followed me, chased after me, tried to corner me, tried to force your
pathetic apology on me—as if I didn't already feel violated enough.
    Boy, if you were sorry,
    you'd never put hands on a woman in the first place.
    You wouldn't 'apologize' just to save face
    after another man had to stop you.

You would have left when I put a palm up between us, running away,
repeating,
    "Leave me alone
    Leave me alone
    Leave me alone
    Leave me alone."

You were never sorry.

I was lucky it didn't go further, that I had a friend with me to make sure nothing else happened. So much luckier than other women have been.

You probably still think it wasn't a big deal.
   It was "just a skirt."
   But you have no idea how violated you made me feel, still feel.
   It's *my* body and *my* skirt,
   and I shouldn't have to be afraid of random men, of being exposed or hurt.

Perfectly Evil

The demands never stop because society demands perfection.

They demand unattainable beauty, use clothes to control, but even more *must be perfect—down to our soul—*

how *perfectly...*

Evil.

Mistakes

No one is perfect, certainly not me; uncertainty controls me.
Listen, I can't make mistakes, too many movie miss-takes,
Miss "takes her human error too seriously"
new meaning to "(un)mistakable."
Seriously, in all sincerity, I sincerely hate messing up.
Lived past lives in trouble, dishonorable.
I dishonor myself with this attitude
because I would never expect perfection from anyone else
or else I'd be sewer-reflection, literal trash, I bash myself.
There I go again, dissing myself again.
I diss my honor, disparage my self-worth
worthless wondering, I (dis)honor my being.
Being too harsh because I've made mistakes. So many mistakes.
But to human is to err.
The phrase for our mishaps is *known* as "human error."
Like an expectation, human reputation for disastrous travesty,
accident-prone, and risky, it's literally recorded scientifically,
and I even breathe air erroneously.
Mistake so humanly, humility owns me
bitch, that's fully me. Error and humanity.

Trying So Hard

I'm trying so hard
    striving so far,
    feeling every single mile, every yard,
but it feels like each step I take
is sunk in mud,
sinking in molasses,
keeping me from being the fastest,
why do I feel each step
like a thousand years,
like time in slow motion,
no notion of progress
despite devotion to progression,
I don't know what lesson
I'm supposed to learn here.
Is this why we fear
change?
But I'm trying to change for the better,
better myself, better my health,
better mindset, go-getter, a healthier goal-setter,
Fuck.
I'm trying SO. HARD.

But maybe slugging through the mud
is what makes the result taste sweet,
makes the victory feel like a feat,
like you're on top of the world,
can't be beat, no sign of defeat,
where struggle and victory meet,
you'll catch me perched in that winner's seat.
Can't say you ever caught me lackin' caught me slackin'
because I fought for each and every win.
You know I'm not bragging,
I'm just finally tagging some self-esteem in.

Shore Up

S hore up your heart, girl.
  Cuz nobody's gunna prop up your chin, girl
  Props to you, girl.
Nobody can hold you up without leaning sideways
And you're tired of side-smiles and half-efforts
And doesn't just everyone love leaning towers
                    without loving the foundation?

You're alone, girl.
  A lone girl.
  On your own, girl, you gotta read what's shown, girl
  You can't beg love from people who promise to be there but aren't really anywhere, well aware of the low you hit, girl.

You can't expect to get what you give, girl. Because too many are already empty.

You don't want to find yourself in the middle of an asthma attack, choking on promises that are air, girl.
  With an inhaler that lacks the power to breathe life back into your constricting airways, girl.

You gotta learn to toss your empty canisters,
Only you are in charge of re-fulfilling.

You're crumbling, girl. And what do they do with crumbling foundation?
    Replace it, deface it without memorial for holding up for so long,
    You'll never be strong enough, girl.
    You'll never BE enough, girl.
    Nobody can fix you
    Nobody can fix you
    Can fix you,
    can fix you,
    can fix,
    you
    can fix
    YOU can fix you.
    You can fix you.

Because you're going to have to.

They'll use your pronoun to beat you down; you can't show weakness,
meekness in this world where it's down to you, girl.

They'll use your gender as a weapon to stab you with, jab you with: "You
fight like a girl, you hit like a girl, you run like a girl."

You're going to turn those 'insults' into results, girl—spike that adrenaline,
    to fight IS to be feminine,
    so much venom in effeminate words, it's so fucking absurd

—make their heads whirl, so when they say, "you fight like a girl,"
    you say

DAMN RIGHT, GIRL.

I Defiantly Care

You say I'm too sensitive,
    need thicker skin,
    like elephants or
knights in armor or
drunks with gin.
You say I'll grow out of this phase,
grow tough to the world,
let things roll off like rain on windows or
hair that's curled.
Like, I haven't been trying for decades
to turn the part of me that cares too much to dust.
And boy, if you think I'll ever become numb,
I don't think you know me very much.
I will care until I'm old with gray hair.
I will care until my body falls apart, and I start to decay.
I will care until my heart runs ragged and palpitates
in my over-empathetic chest.
You think they've gotten the best of me,
when really, though imperfectly,
I'm just trying so hard to be the best me.

I'm Just a Girl

I'm just a girl
Living in this burning world,
Trying to take care of myself
But also everyone else.
It's so overwhelming
Anxiety twisting my gut,
But I am trying my best.
I'm really, really, truly trying my best.

Fucking Sunflower

L isten.
      I am a delicate fucking sunflower, OKAY?
      My insides are as soft as misted breath on windows.
My soul is as soft as feathery pillows.
I am so pathetically, entirely breakable.
And I so badly crave a gentleness I can't fully explain
I can't fully define
I want divine softness
Trust this, I don't even understand this myself.
I think there's a reason I turn to hurt/comfort tropes in fiction.
I received the hurt but didn't get the comfort,
and now I'm chasing it like the one that got away.
I'm chasing it like a dog with a bone.
I'm chasing it even though I'm no longer really alone.
I crave softness like it's a substance,
but this one's safe for use.
Please.
Just be gentle with me.
I don't think I can take any more hurt, really.
Because I am a delicate fucking sunflower, OKAY?

My Scribbles

I'll start publishing my scribbles
my scraggles and rumbles, and doodles.

Stop caring so damn much about perfection,
stop stalling for mediocre porridge because I'm delusional enough
to think it needs to be "just right."
Art doesn't have to be polished or lukewarm or room temperature.
It can be messy, scalding, or as freezing as the tundra.

Perfection is a reflection of insecurity,
a deflection of my own deficiency and inefficiency.
There's perfection in imperfection,
a rejection of societal impression.

Why should I care about what every single person thinks of me?
Of my art?
The people it's meant for will find it,
so I won't hide it.
Can't gatekeep it until it's polished for mass consumption
because it's not.

It's for me, and anyone else who feels too deeply.
Anyone else who has killed themselves for the "perfect" myth,
only to find it unattainable.
And not as desirable as we're led to believe.
I find it so admirable when people are unabashedly themselves,
with their art out on their sleeve.

Instagram Spoken

Spoken Version: https://www.instagram.com/reel/DQpH7ZpkSi3/?
utm_source=ig_web_copy_link&igsh=NTc4MTIwNjQ2YQ==

Perfection Kills Individuality

Do not kill individuality
human originality,
belligerent nonconformity,
unique personality,
personal, inherent creativity,
creatively customized reality
modified appearance commodity.
Why would you all want to be the same, anyway?
Is it driven by uncertainty?
Certainly, you can see creativity adds to society.
Insecurity? Anxiety?
Afraid nothing makes you special,
so you kill specialty.
Replace humans with robots artificially.
Trade wearable glitter for stiffened suits
starch and pressed
a stark pretense.
If you're boring,
just fucking say that.

All of Me

Rumi asked, "Why couldn't you love me?"
   But that wasn't it, not what got me,
   Not what gave me pause,
It was
It was
When she said, "All of me."

"Why couldn't you love all of me?"

Why...
   Why *couldn't* you love all of me?
   My god, why do you look at me so differently?
   Like I'm an alien, subhuman, 'other' category,
   Categorically make me feel like a mistake
   Like being born
   Existing,
   my very existence is out of place.
   No place to fit in, off step, off pace, wrong in my own skin, every step a sin,
   out of sync, on the edge, on the brink, not the same, you taught me shame...
   I'm ashamed.

Why couldn't you love all of me?
    ALL of me?
    All OF me?
    All of ME?
    What could possibly be so wrong with me?
    Life taught me to hide, cover up, wear a mask,
    I can only be me privately, quietly, secretly, make-up for society—priority
propriety.

I want to be like Rumi,
    Rejecting half-loves and conditional care,
    Belting ballads of self-acceptance and love
    Embracing ME and the people who are *there*.
    Who love
    her for her
    Me for me
    Unconditionally.
    I want to reconcile my own harmony
    Technicolor thoughts spilling freely,
    Sharp edges glowing symbolically.

I want to embrace my darkness and my scars,
    my flaws, visible and invisible.
    If you can't love all of me…
    then I will.
    No matter how long it takes,
    I will learn to love all of myself wholeheartedly.

All of me, imperfectly.

~Inspired by the movie *KPop Demon Hunters* (2025)

The Evils of Silencing and Erasure

O ne of the biggest evils we've faced is how our society erased us—our discoveries, ingenuity, studies—furthermore, how they still fight to silence our voices.

Keep us focused on shallow things and horizontal hostilities.

If we're not impossibly beautiful
  AND dressed 'appropriately'
  AND literally perfect,
  why should we exist at all?

Shrink down, shrink until you're small.
  They'll try to control how you look in the same eye that defies seeing you;
  squints to make you invisible.

Loud Silence

When they say silence is louder than words,
Remember:
You cannot NOT communicate.
No answer *is* an answer.
And that's how the silence says it all.

Disappearing Again

I'm disappearing again...
    Wrapping isolation around myself like a cocoon
    only, I'm not sure if this is for transformation.
Will I come out differently on the other side?
Gain my wings?
Bloom into something fluttery and lovely?
Somehow, I doubt it.
You're disappearing again
Like disappearing ink
a mere facade.

Erase Me

So, they want me to write an erasure poem—
Erased phrases creating poetic meaning.
Use felt on chalkboard letter outlines to wipe words away until
nothing is left but chalk stains.

Imagine that. People wanting a woman erased.

As if women haven't spent centuries being erased—from poetry, from
literature, from history, from voting, from basic human rights, from serious
issues on this Earth.

Reduced to possessions—obsessions with image
No value other than in body, in clothing, in handbags.

As if women's voices aren't already silenced enough, they want me to erase
my own words—they want me to personally erase each word myself—they
don't care what I say; they do not want to hear my voice today.

So, they want me
Erased. creating
chalk outlines, nothing is left but
stains.
People wanting a woman erased.
Women spent centuries erased—

120

from basic human rights, from this Earth.
In body bags.
Women's voices silenced, erase my own
words—they want me to personally erase each word myself—they don't
care what I say;
they do not hear my voice today.

They want me
Erased.
chalk- outlines,
women
in body -bags
silenced
erase, own
words, want me to erase myself—I say
not today.

The Disappearing Girl

In fiction, I don't like "The Disappearing Girl."

Come One, Come All; Appearing for the First Five minutes—The Amazing,
The Bold and Alive, "Disappearing Girl!"

Get addicted to her disappearing act, addiction to her departure has warped
her purpose for being there in the first place—

Poof, she's gone! Without a trace!

Would You Take A Look At That!

It only took *this long* for my poem to erase her—erasure is shrinking women
until they have no place, until they vanish—and that's not a metaphor.

I fear erasure.
 I want to yell: I AM HERE!

I am alive, I breathe air, I take up space, and I refuse to disappear.
 I am here.
 Not a mystery, not your puzzle piece, or plot device to teach a lesson.

I am a person, not a vanishing act.

Fiction is meant to entertain, but I am not entertainment, and I am not entertained.

History is already filled with disappearing atrocities,
   so why should our fiction also have to be?
   Enough real women have disappeared, figuratively AND physically.

So, Come One, Come All! Have An Eye Or Ear To Lend?
   Watch the real magic trick:

I stick around until

The End.

Just Your Voice

Ursula the Sea Witch had it right:

You don't need to shout to be heard.

Even without a voice

The right people are still listening.

Much Me

I'm sorry for sharing so much of me
   I fear it's too much of me
   If I give you more me
In bite-sized pieces,
Will it make me more palatable?
Make me more compatible
With whatever unwritten requirements
Come with your compliments?
Or even
You giving a single damn?

Ballerina Farm

So, you've farmed yourself a ballerina.
    Restricting her pirouettes
    Fading her life
Until she's just dancing silhouettes.
Only shadows in backgrounds,
A watered-down version
Muted sounds.
You've farmed your ballerina.
You must be *so proud.*

So. You've farmed yourself a ballerina.
    What's next?
    To the slaughterhouse?
    To the butcher block?
    What other good can your ballerina be, if not a trapped spouse?
    If you don't have her on lock, locked down
    Locked away
    Never to see the light of day
    The light of stages
    Of curtain calls, applause, and adoration
    Only locked-up cages

SO. You've *farmed* your ballerina.
   And I wonder
   Do you love her as much now
   As when she was allowed to dance?
   And did you forget
   That you were the one who forbade her? Who made her stop?
   Don't you dare demand your ballerina stop dancing
   After all

You farmed your ballerina, cultivated her,
   Knew exactly who and what she was before you planted your seeds.
   And though your farm and rage-bait may be fake,
   do you know how many women actually suffer this fate?
   She's not a trope or cosplay; this is so many women's reality.

You *wanted* the ballerina—the free spirit, the artist, tutu, on toe pointe,
twirling, swirling, spinning, lost in the symphony and beat
   They wanted a *ballerina*;
   Was it just to stop her feet?

Heartbreakingly Evil

They'll take you, erase you, convince you that pain is the only love you deserve.

Love En Pointe

L ove shouldn't hurt,
　　but my goodness, I love you to agony.
　　The heart in me
pounds for you
beats for you,
dances to the rhythm of your heart
like it's your prima ballerina assoluta.
I've never loved anyone to the pointe of hurting
love ballet en pointe
gorgeous dancer
pointe work all the way down up on my toes
damn if that doesn't hurt.
My heart pirouettes for you,
spinning in circles,
dizzy with all the feelings I held
because I didn't want to burden you.
So much already on your plate,
the world on your shoulders,
how could I not shoulder you, too?
How could my heart not dance for you?

Serrated Love

Y ou taught me love like a blade teaches skin, delicately at first,
then all at once, you're bleeding because those first few layers of
skin are just too thin.

You taught me through crude jokes at my expense that my skin needed to be
thicker,
    but it's hard to grow tough when you're battling for love and your opponent
is liquor.

The blade teaches flesh that it is weak
    The blade teaches flesh to be meek
    The blade teaches flesh pain, inch by inch
    The blade teaches flesh to flinch.

You taught torment, terror, trial
    It's no wonder learning love has taken a while.

I've had to unlearn your sharpened version, my aversion to a cutting love.
    I've abandoned your love's teaching,
    reaching my own conclusions of what love should really be.

I've concluded your love is convoluted, suited to no one, especially not me.
  I've concluded the love you alluded to is not love at all, not really.
  I've concluded that true love is so incredibly, impossibly soft. Gentle. Easy.

So soft, it's sugary
  sweet and fluffy like a feathery pillow, or sugar-coated candy.
  My conclusions have superseded your conceited illusions of love.
  So while your sandstone-sharpened knife may have carved life lessons into my skin,
  you certainly did not teach me love,
  and though I'm scarred, scared, and flinch,
  I forsake your twisted love, and you will never fucking win.

Colorblind

You made me stop writing for a while,
time I can never get back,
time's sand slipping through a crack.
You're uninspired, like gray-scale coloring books,
colorblind in your ego and pretension
with knife-hands drawing blood
every time you seek love attention.
The problem with only seeing in black and white
is mistaking blood for water.
If you can't see red, how can you know your butcher-hands just slaughter?
When you refuse to see perspectives,
can't even think through action-reaction consequences,
how do you know to stop killing?
You killed my creativity, drew blood from me
with serrated fingertips,
spilled what you saw as water from my core,
swore you'd always love me through text,
yet always left me sore.

Case Study of Feminism and 3OH!3

‎❧

I want to write a case study
    on the relationship between feminism and hating the band 3OH!3.

You flaunted your college essay, like brownie points could win your degree.
Claimed 3OH!3 is sexist; it was your thesis.

You refused to listen, but hang on, I'm confused...
    Because what do you mean, "The lyrics 'don't trust a ho' are sexist,"
    but *not* you, performing mental gymnastics trying to bend my "no"??
    Did you get confused between essay and SA?
    Is feminism just better as a construct for you?

Abstract, distant, a nice contemplation,
    your performative condemnation of misogyny.
    Sure, the song may be sexist, but admit you're a hypocrite.
    Face reality, you don't even practice what your thesis preaches.

"DONTTRUSTME" is on my favorite playlist,
    blasting in my car, screaming at the top of my lungs, "DON'T TRUST A
HO!!!!!!!!!!!!"

Because who do you think you are?
I'm petty—I'll dance to it out of spite
because it's my right to take back the word ho,
and take back my right to the word "no."

It's a bop of a song I rock out to happily,
   as vigorously as I never fucked you,
   and you know what?
   Even screaming about the hos, I'm still a damn feminist,
   because I don't *perform* an equality-bit;
   I don't just *say* I respect women,
   I fucking do it.

Blind Want

Don't let your "want" blind you.
    You want love
        enough to turn a blind eye, blindly falling,
ignoring flags of red dye
born of want.
You want *this* love to be *the* love of your life.
You can ignore entire atrocities
wreaked from pretty hands your want-eyes won't see.

At this point, you're not in a relationship with another person;
    you're exclusive with your want.
    Who you *want* them to be.
    How you *want* them to treat you.
    The feelings you want them to see and return.
    You're fighting for a relationship with your want.

Want will make you stay,
    when you know damn well you shouldn't.
    Want will let you pay, will let you say, "They wouldn't. Couldn't."
    But what does your wanting know?
    Your wanting knows longing

your wanting knows pining
your wanting knows unrequited craving
your wanting knows forever waiting and sighing.
Your want will keep you abused, keep you used
because you refused to see your wanting for what it is.

You're in love with your want, not the monster who haunts your bed.
Your want will get you dead.
Your want will never make someone good
and
if someone is good,
they will never make you want.
Because you'll already have.

Fire Drill

When we were little, and we had "fire drills," they drilled us to save ourselves.
If you hear that alarm:
Get out.
...I hear that alarm.

Don't stop for belongings—lead your loved ones out—don't stop—don't look back
until you're out.

I like to think toxic relationships are much the same.

No, you don't have to be dating for this fire to start,
after all,
most flames are an *uncontained accident*—

You didn't mean to leave the stove on,
you just forgot it was something *dangerous*.

They drilled us to save ourselves:
When you hear the alarm, get out, don't doubt yourself; just leave.

You don't know if the flames will get worse—you don't know if there will be an explosion:
Get out.

But with relationships…
sometimes you don't hear the alarm…
Sometimes the flame can be mistaken for warmth
and you don't know the smoke filling your lungs isn't a drug of love,
you don't realize it's poisoning you—suffocating you—you just thought
you couldn't catch your breath around them, and that's *so*… addicting.

They drilled us to save ourselves:
But sometimes that alarm sounds like fireworks
and that fire feels like passion,
and that smoke is like the next hit you've been waiting to inhale, it's *so*.
Addicting.

They drilled us to save ourselves:
But that fire against my skin is the only thing that hurts worse than how
you make me feel inside, and I have to decide if being burned alive is worth it
or if I should do as I was taught and get out—

Because I *hear* that alarm

And I don't want to be stuck inside your *burning house.*

When Eminem rapped about leaving out the window, being called "window-pain," I don't think he understood the person *jumping*.
Forget stop, drop, and roll—I want to *shatter* your windows
and jump from your ledge—

The only good thing about you
is that you make

painful poetry pour profusely, painting pages poetically perfect.

You volcanic person.

Loving you was never about the eruptions
    it wasn't about the fire or heat
    it was about your dormancy.
    How long I could stand at your base and live in your calm.

They drilled us to save ourselves.

But a fire is the only time I have ever been taught self-preservation.

Instagram Spoken

Spoken Version: https://www.instagram.com/reel/C_S5M33JPMn/?
utm_source=ig_web_copy_link&igsh=NTc4MTIwNjQ2YQ==

I'm the Storm

I need to be the storm

for all the times I've felt powerless,

because man has yet to conquer the weather.

Sure,

you can weather the storm,

but you can't storm the weather.

I'll Love You Through Storms

I 'll love you through storms.
    Or at least… I'll love the idea of you.
    I'll love you through hurricanes, rains, downpours,
I can only love the idea of you.

Of course, I'm not yours, and you're not mine
    and that's fine, I wouldn't want to confine you,
    and you can't force me here, don't fear the storm, stand in it.

I'll love you through earthquakes, even if it breaks me,
    the idea of you is a natural disaster,
    I'll love you faster than the earth can split—hit me with the idea of you.
    Like the universe, I can't see all of you,
    but like howling winds, you are there and physical and present
    but invisible…
    …I'm hesitant.

The elephant in the room
    is that you thought you were my whirlwind, a twister, tornado, typhoon—
    meant to sweep me off my feet.
    And my darling…

That's so terribly sweet.

But I am the monsoon, tsunami, tidal wave
    crashing down your shores.
    Downpours are nothing compared to my ferocity, velocity winds
    devastation so destructive, drowning your doors,
    you can try to shake me, but know you'll never take me;
    I am unattainable.

I'll love you through storms;
    We are the hot and cold currents clashing
    I'll love you through storms,
    winds lashing,
    lightning flashing,
    my waves crashing,
    people dashing,

I'll love you through storms.

Even if we are the ones creating them.

Gifting Forgiveness

The gift of forgiving is for me, not you.

When I forgive, it's like the leaves in autumn, colors blooming in death; I let hurts bloom in vibrant shades before letting them fall from dead branches.

My forgiveness is this frigid winter's ice.

The snow blanketing a frozen ground.

Fresh. Cold. Pure.

The gift of my forgiveness is to thaw my own frozen heart…

because I don't want to be trapped in winter forever.

I let go of old hurts like dead leaves

so my branches can bloom in spring again.

The gift of forgiving is just like the changing seasons.

I can change with the weather

I can let go

I can forgive, but I won't forget, just like the oldest tree.

I'll hold the memories inside me, and grieve each falling leaf.

I might forgive the hurt,

but the gift of my forgiveness is for *me*.

I don't forgive your actions.

I don't forgive the pain you caused.

But… I do forgive myself for feeling all my grief.

Hearts Aren't Meant for Breaking

A heart isn't meant for breaking,
   for taking and smashing
   for faking and laughing
for ruse, use, and lose.
My heart was never meant for breaking…
yet it's beaten, battered, and bruised from all the violence you choose.
Despite its bloody state, somehow, it's still beating.

Because a heart isn't meant for breaking, forsaking, and flaking.
   A heart is meant for making rhythmic life.
   A heart is the balance and flow, the drum and the bow;
   a heart knows where the blood should go.

My heart knows where the blood should go.
   To pump gently through my body.
   A heart is meant for love—caring, life-sustaining love.
   So, no.
   A heart isn't meant for breaking.
   My heart is meant for making—
   Making poems, making blood, making breathtaking love.
   ~Making~

Love in Friendship

I t took me a while, longer than I'd like to admit,
    to understand
    there is love in friendship.
My view of love was skewed, skewered like meat on a stick.
Chopped up, run through, my view on love was sick.
I was taught I had to earn love;
couldn't get it just because I gave it
couldn't hear it just because I spoke it.

I could earn love through apologies, sorries, and self-sacrifices.
    These devices might earn a return on love, then.
    Transactional when, in actuality, it should have been free.
    I hurt a friend because I couldn't see how they could actually love me
without a fee.
    Insisted they quit the word, rejected the "love,"
    because it's not something I'd heard unromantically.
    I'm sorry about that.
    I wasn't used to a love that didn't hurt because I thought that was the love
I'd earned.

My friends today

have taught me 'love' more accurately,
have loved me so gently, so acutely.
I'm still not the best with love,
but I've grown exponentially, potentially exceeding my love-expectation.
Starting to disbelieve love has expiration.

My friends' love is my inspiration.
You inspire me entirely, tirelessly, so lovingly.
I only hope I can show my love in its entirety.
So, sincerely, thank you,
for showing love so admirably.

~For Shelby, Sammy, Dani C., Doraly, Helen, and Michelle

Loving You

L oving you
has been earth-shattering.
I thought I knew love like the back of my hand,
thought I knew it like my favorite route home,
like a safety drill for natural disasters.

But practice is so much different from experience,
so how could I possibly have prepared
for the earthquake that is you?
You shook my world and loved my faults.
You made me realize, damn, nobody has ever actually loved me before.
You gently shook my radars and more.

Loving you has been one of the most important things I've done,
because I never knew how badly
I'd want to make sure nobody else ever hurt you.
And I know I chose a violent metaphor,
but how else can I explain the way you shook my belief core?
How you destroyed the city of self-hate I'd let others build up in me.
How you fell buildings in the lie of love I'd been accepting,

the love-pain I thought I deserved.

I picked a jarring metaphor
   because it really was earth-shattering…
   To be loved so fucking softly.
   So, let me rephrase.
   Being loved BY you has been earth-shattering.
   And all I can do is keep loving you
   in soft, trembling, quaking return.

~For David

The Weather Is Nice Today

The weather is so nice today.
    I want to treasure you,
      spoil you without measure, too.
Treat you with the softness we both missed.
I gaze at you in fondness.

In a world full of pain,
    I'm dying to be your kindest kindness.
    Your kind of softness,
    and maybe I should love less,
    but at least you know you're not loveless.
    In this life of hurt,
    I want to be the one who makes you hurt less.

Practice gentleness in soft words and light touches.
    Practice calm everywhere the light touches.
    I look around, seeing people hurt each other, and I think,
    why?
    In a life that's hard enough,
    I don't want to make it any tougher.

I want to be your wind, the breeze, your air;
    I want to be your ease, your tree.
    You are my vacation home retreat,
    my comfort, relaxation,
    way to unwind,
    hang out,
    maybe even *escape.*
    I really *"Want so BAD"* to be the same.

Let me be your forest for rest,
    don't worry about the rest.
    I'll delicately cup your hands in mine
    with so much tenderness
    you're left without a doubt that everything will be just fine.
    Because after all,
    the weather is so nice today.

~Inspired by words from Lee Minho (aka Lee Know)

Violently Evil

S ociety is so strange; people are confused.
   They've villainized the oppressed, poor, and abused.
   They've pointed fingers and accused,
declaring evil of the wrong people.
When the true evil is right here in front of us, amused,
sitting in positions of power, laughing at those they've used.
The real evil is physical, political, religious, and systemic violence.

Portraits and Mirrors

I am only destructive

When I am painted as such.

If you want me constructive,

Put down your red brush.

If you paint the blood I've not yet spilled,

I'll become the horror your art has willed.

Don't capture my portrait monstrous

or I'll frame myself a mirror.

The Ballad of The Bad Boy

This is The Ballad of The Bad Boy:
    Why do we criticize girls who romanticize the 'Bad Boy'?
    I fantasize about leather jackets, tattoos, and bedroom eyes;
it's no surprise, swallow white lies.

Let's discuss "Nice Guy's" disguise.
    Nice Guy *says* he's nice,
    but his nice comes at a price—priceless.
    He wants *me* to get to know *him,*
    show me how impressive he is; the pleasure is all his.
    He just wants to jump, pump, and dump,
    pounce, flounce, and bounce;
    'Nice Guy' wants to own you and bone you.

He says I'm "pretty enough to get him off" — so off-putting!
    And when I'm offended by his offer (wanting to tell him to fuck off),
    somehow, not wanting to be his booty call, at his beck and call,
    makes me a bitch, which he calls me when I say, "No, thank you."
    Because he says I'm "not that pretty anyway,"
    he could "do better any day," and I'm just a "dumb slut."

But you know what?

    Bad Boy knows that's not the way to get a lady to layyy—in bed.

    How to get "a-head."

    Bad Boy might love me and leave me,

    but at least he'll leave me *satisfied*,

    make me feel like I've TESTIFIED!

Bad Boy has never called me a name or made me feel shame.

    He makes me feel desirable, inspirable;

    we both receive,

    no reprieve,

    best believe he doesn't want to be tied down,

    but he'll tie you down in the most delicious of ways.

    Who says I need a ring to be worth something to someone, anyway?

Give me intentional tension

    Taste tangled

    Intertwined in confines

    that bind and blind, lose loose minds,

    Shaking, shivering, shuddering with pressure, pleasure, erotic without measure

    Until we're both spent.

Bad Boy… is about *consent*.

    He'll prevent hurting you by reading the content of your body cues.

    He won't try to keep going if you say, "I don't know…"

    Because HE knows:

    ~ENTHUSIASM EQUALS ORGASM~

Hesitation means check in with me, bro—hey, slow your roll, chill your dick,

    stop, drop, and rewind, do you mind,

    give me a second or two, this moment is not just about *you*.

We throw the 'Bad Boy' label around based on an image; imagine if we based it on common decency.

So yeah, I like the Bad Boys—you know—the ones with a reputation for being good in bed.
Being *good*—kind—compassionately passionate
because I'd rather be loved the right way for one day
than the wrong ways for the rest of my days.

Yes.
Both guys want sex.
The difference is fucking respect.

Instagram Spoken

Spoken Version: https://www.instagram.com/reel/C_Vido6uRUZ/?
utm_source=ig_web_copy_link&igsh=NTc4MTIwNjQ2YQ==

Take Back the Night

So many women I know.
   So many women I know have had their innocence taken
   confidence shaken.
So many women I know whose "NO"
wasn't good enough.
It is a sad day when I am afraid to walk alone.

It is a sad day when every parent has to teach their daughters to be afraid to walk alone,
   and sadly, it's not the unknown that's feared.
   I used to think that the only monsters in the night came from under unmade beds
   I never knew that at night you could be unmade in a monster's made-up bed.

So many women I know—
   We are taught that it's up to *us* not to *give* them a reason.
   But what reason is ever reasonable for raping someone?

We live in a society that embraces rape culture,
   cries "WHORE" at Miley Cyrus

while applauding Robin Thicke.
Teach little girls "not to be like her"
while singing along with him,
while your little him is listening to *you*.

We are teaching our sons that 'blurred lines' are glorified,
    that consent doesn't matter, no matter what she says, she really wants it.
    As a matter of fact, the most important matter boys should be taught
    is that women matter.
    Women's choices matter.

So many women I know,
    and so many men... I don't.
    And to those men, I want to walk up like a reckoning.
    They will know me by the storm in my eyes,
    the crash in my step, and
    by my lightning-struck scream,
    and I will scream:

"How could you? Don't you care what you've taken from her?!
    Scars etched so deep she will feel them for years to come,
    scars etched down so deep into veins,
    tracing up arms,
    flowing into hearts until
    pump-pumps out poison.
    Pump-pumps out mistrust.
    Pump-pumps out pain and self-loathing.

How pathetic are you that you had to *take* what you can't *get?*
    Was scarring her worth a few moments of your conquer-control-personal-
pleasure? Pathetic."

So many women I know

and these words are for them.
It is a hard thing to say… but I am afraid of men.

I have faced more than my fair share of domestic violence,
I know what it is to be scared.
Truly scared.
Flashbacks, like a PTSD soldier,
only I fought not a war but an onslaught.

So many women I know
but the only war they ever fought was for the rights to their own bodies
and—
we lost.
We lost our battles.
But not this war.

And that is why we must take back the night,
for so many brave, strong, courageous, inspirational women I know
and the millions of other women… I don't know.
The ones you know.

6

~Dedicated to the "Take Back the Night" event that asked me to write this poem and

every person who has shared their story with me.

Doll Face

The movie *Birds of Prey* had me SCREAMING
This movie moved me: Harley Quinn—you win 2020, honey.

Has anyone ever exemplified exactly what it entails to escape more exquisitely? This isn't just a breakup,
wake up,
this is the cycle of abuse.
Our bad bitch is finally breaking loose from 'puddin' and the sexual exploitation synonymous with feminine liberation—not to mention the 'sex-pectation' of her 'crazy' reputation.

I want to be as dramatic as this diva,
driving trucks into toxic industries—bailing before burning.
Girl, you burn those bridges, break those bones, break those knees,
do whatever you motherfucking please.
Make me sway, queen, *slay*.
Diamonds are a girl's best friend, and weren't you just crushed coal until you shone, you boss bitch?
SWAY.

The absolute most poignant part of this film is the physical representation

of four traumatized women holding on to a young girl,
    bringing her back behind their backs,
    bodies becoming barriers, barricades, blockades,
    braving bats, beatings, gun barrels, ba(rrr)ages of bullets, bombs, blood,
    battlefield-battered bodies bearing the brunt of brutality
    as women so often do.

It was beautiful to see these bad bitches break bones,
    sling back bullet for bullet, blow for blow,
    because we are not just punching bags, shooting ranges, bullseye.
    We hit back.

And here's Harley Quinn, a 'villain,'
    a 'crazy criminal'
    making sure it doesn't happen to another girl.

If you think this movie is just an empty gesture to appease women, that Harley is just a jester, then,

doll face—the joke's on you.

Trickle, Recycle, Abuse

Trickle-down economics is a fountain
    that was never really meant to flow,
    never meant to water and grow people outside the basin.
No.

"Trickle-down" is a beautiful connotation of a phrase
    invoking images of raindrops on windows,
    or fountains spraying water through the air, but that's not fair.
    Because fountains are essentially pools, pooling resources, pooling water
to reuse,
    refuse to care, refuse to share, give no refuge, let the poor drink the air.
    We're fools.

Fountain water will never nourish grass.
    That same recycled water will fountain through the sky for all to see, all to
view,
    as the water trickles, only for a few.
    Never meant to touch or take, drink or taste.
    And when that water is murky and mucky, maybe then the grass will get
fed.
    If it's not already dead.

Environmentally, practically, and morally: The fountain is a failure.
    You can die of thirst, but we waste water like we're rich with it, like it's
infinite.

But you know what? I'm fucking parched.

Can't quench my thirst, like a vampire baited with a bucket of banned blood,
    saliva floods my mouth, watering, salivating until dehydrating.
    Desperation clawing up my throat,
    thirst beyond comprehension,
    pulse point palpitation, tension, apprehension, suspension
    thirst overtaking,
    dry aching inflames my jaw, raw hunger gnaws until fangs burst from my
gums.
    Starvation overcomes, more animal than human,
    sharpened canines evolve to drink water like a carnivore from the gore of
life's blood.

Your trickle-down fountain failed to keep me watered,
    my cup is empty,
    too far down at the bottom to gather pitiful, trickling, pitiful, used-up
drops of blood,
    more mud now than water.

Water is a human right.

People will not lie down and die, docile, without a fight.
    Who are you
    to play god with lives?

If your fountain will not feed us in your gluttonous hoarding,
    then I will use these fangs forged by a failing fountain to take what I need
to live forcibly.

Look what you've made of me.

Desperation drives desperate deeds,
    and every action is met with an opposed equal reaction
    and I oppose your action of resource thievery.

You've more than shown you don't see us equally,
    so don't be surprised that your greed made an enemy, animosity.
    I see why you don't want equality.
    Almost like you *know* you're behaving unethically.
    So don't cry when we match fucking bloodsucking energy.
7 & 8

~Dedicated to Angelique @mootsupplications for the prompt: "fangs forged by a failing fountain."

Instagram Spoken

Spoken Version: https://www.instagram.com/reel/DMRbkOxsxgC/?
utm_source=ig_web_copy_link&igsh=NTc4MTIwNjQ2YQ==

Nothing to Impugn

⬥

She said, "Do not impugn our integrity."
　　As if the man were the one in the wrong...

　　But miss ma'am, miss lady,
you'd have to have *any*.
With pretty words and broken promises,
your integrity is empty;
nothing here to see.
Your integrity is invisible; transparently missing.
Meaning: You sure don't show any.

The 'good person' you've made up in your head
　　is no different than a child's imaginary friend.
　　Deluded yourself into thinking you have moral superiority,
　　but colluded to spit on the minority,
　　a convoluted definition of integrity, definitely not denotative.

When your actions don't match your words, your integrity is for the birds.
　　That old-school reference is just for you, by the way, so you'd actually
comprehend it.
　　So far past your prime, it's actually a crime to hold a seat at a table

you no longer EAT at,
never ATE at,
(you'll have to ask your Gen Z staff about that triple entendre).

I think you confused the word 'integrity' with 'wealthy.'
They both end in Y, I guess?

When you show active harm to another human being,
any morality or integrity you've preached is just a reach,
you've reached,
you're reaching,
look at the fucked-up shit you're teaching.
When you show active harm to your neighbor,
no matter how much YOU hate their skin or religion,
their accent or orientation—and we know you hate them,
as you've hurt them without hesitation.
When you show active harm, you show exactly who you really are.

And: We. See. You.
We've seen how you've voted over the years, you sly fox.
Integrity is not a self-assigned label.
It shows in what we've seen you say and do,
and lady,
in your every action, word, and syllable;
your integrity is so tragically far from unimpugnable.

Of Breath and Bone

❦

I am made of sorrow and rage,
    of fragile flesh and hard-hitting heartbeats.
    I see hatred spewed in this country from polluted politicians and
bloated billionaires.

And I wonder why, with our bodies made of the same damn elements, we
see life so fucking differently.

As if
    we are not all made up the same elementally,
    as if
    we are not all made of the same humanity.
    Why are *we* over-pouring with humility, while the richest only over-pour
vanity?
    It's insanity.
    I can't imagine wishing ill on others just for existing, without sound
reasoning, with extreme prejudice,
    not as an act of revenge, vengeance, or injustice.

We are all the same fundamentally,
    made of tragic life and death,
    made of emotion and symmetry,

of breath and bone;
we are made of the same damn tragedy.

But that's where commonality ends... theirs is the tragedy of the commons,
and yeah, that's so fucking common—both prevalent *and* vulgar—the
audacious unoriginality.
While ours is the tragedy of desperately craving to just live happily.
Peacefully.
In these bodies made of elements, we know will decay and return to dirt
indiscriminately.

TikTok Spoken

Spoken Version: https://www.instagram.com/reel/DQNd_HkAXJr/?
utm_source=ig_web_copy_link&igsh=NTc4MTIwNjQ2YQ==

You, Evil Thing

Y ou,
      made of love and sugar-sweet goodness.
      You were never evil,
just a woman, a human, beautiful, divine, goddess;
they should beg your forgiveness.

Marie Antoinette never coined, "Let them eat cake."
   Elizabeth Báthory never tried, yet confined until she died.

Hekate, help me, goddess of moon and magic, work your will, hold the torch,
protect and light the way
   Lilith, dark moon resistance of the night, help me rebel, wreak havoc, claim
independence
   Both connect me to my feminine energy.

Feminine power is demonized,
   while the patriarchy is weaponized.

Sure, there are evil queens in history, but not every single one
   and witches are literally mythology
   but Salem-mass-hysteria has shown the dangers of religious zealotry.

You,
  lovely girl,
  beautiful woman, trans or cis,
  gorgeous they;
  no matter your color or sexuality,
  no matter whether you have a disability,
  no matter what they claim, no matter what they say:
  You were never the evil thing in this tale.
  You were just trying to live, to survive each day.

You,
  Evil Thing,
  I wish for you to embrace your power; be empowered.
  Keep striving for every hope and dream—be filled with advocacy.
  Let no one destroy your majesty, after all;
  You're a goddamn queen.

~Dedicated to the Evil Things

Credits

Collaborations:

- Mother Earth: written with Doraly
- Cracked Glass and Mirrors: written with Eric Tu (aka: Tu the Judoka)
- Beastly Beautiful: written with Shelby Ann Love (@Inkingteatroll)

Acknowledgments

I can't possibly thank everyone as I'm so thankful for everyone who is supportive and loves my poetry, so thank you to everyone who read this <3

(That being said, my thanks are a bit long, sorrrryyyy!)

Thank you to my matriarchy: Tracey, my singing and dancing mom. Carolyn, my plant-loving and crafting grandma. My great-grandma Tracey Jewel, who is my middle namesake. Corine, my joking and sweet aunt. And my great-aunt Nona, who recently passed, for gifting me a poetry book for Christmas when I was young; thank you for beginning my love of poetry—and I still have that book with her signature.

I have a beautiful text from her about my first book that I want to share in honor of her memory: "Hello Kristen! Congratulations!! Your mom was here visiting, sharing your published book. Wow!! We are so proud of you. Keep writing! Love you! <3"—Aunt Nona

Thank you to my love, David, for aggressively supporting me and my dreams. He's in my corner no matter what, and it means the entire world to me. He's so enthusiastic about my passions, and I really think he believes I can do anything. You're the bee's knees, and I love you!

Thank you to my primordial ooze twin, Shelby, for letting me talk her ever-living ear off about this book and all of my poetry. She's another one who aggressively supports me, and I wouldn't have it any other way. Thank you for not only writing a spoken collaboration with me, but for allowing me to use it in this collection <3 She's the cover artist for my first book, *More Than Half-Drowning*!

Thank you to my friend Sammy, who told me my poetry was the most relatable and understandable she's ever heard. That's honestly the best compliment anyone could give me. And thank you to her husband, Jeff, who came with her to my first book-release event. The support from these two is SO wholesome and filled with love.

Thank you to my friend Doraly for endlessly supporting me and my poetry. She is wildly encouraging and truly a gem. Thank you for writing collaborations with me and allowing me to use one in this book! She is my ARC reader, and I so appreciate how much she's helped me. She encourages me to promote myself, and I can't wait until she releases a book so I can do the same for her.

Thank you to my friend Eric Tu (aka Tu the Judoka) for helping (and convincing) me to organize a book-release event for my first book at the Xia Gallery & Cafe (a huge thanks to them for hosting my event there). Thank you for collaborating with me and allowing me to use one of our collaborations in this book. Another collaboration we've done is in his book, "Space Channel 612." His book is amazing; everyone should check it out!

Thank you to Mollie Lacy for also being so lovely and supportive. They came to feature and read poetry at my first release, and I really love their work. Their poems are so deep and just gorgeous. As soon as their book is back in print, I'll share that link so fast.

Thank you to one of my Stay friends, Sienna, who not only allowed me to use her original art for my book promotion but also donated extra stickers to give away! I adore her art; you can find her stickers @StayStickerShop on Etsy, Instagram, and TikTok. She makes delightful content, and she is an absolute light in this world. Definitely follow her for all the positivity and joy she radiates. (**Link Below[1]**)

Thank you to my friend Dani C. for reminding me to give myself grace when I'm trying to do way too much at once. She supports me so much and has really encouraged me for this book. She's an inspirational person, and one day I will convince her to paint a book cover :P (she's a wonderful artist). I hope I show her even half as much love as she shows me.

Thank you to my friends Tyler and Chris for being so sweet and so caring.

They come to my spoken word events and cheer me on way more than I deserve <3 They came to my first book release with the sweetest gift of their travel ducks!!!! (iykyk)

Thank you to all of my family for being so supportive of my books. Dani, Kyle, and Magnus for sending me flowers at my first poetry release and making it so special and memorable. My cousin Alexis for buying my book and making me sign it (haha—I swear I'm giving it back so soon).

Thank you to a few of my speech role models: Amorette, Gayle, and LaRoyce. I'll always be thankful to you all for helping me find my voice and being absolute dynamite women to look up to.

Thank you to my Instagram poetry community (way too many to list), but I'll list a few. The goddesses! Beautiful souls inside and out. Michelle, who leaves me the sweetest comments on my poetry and gives endless love. She's an animal activist, and her poetry is so important. Helen, who encourages my spoken word and shows up for me no matter what. She's not only a fantastic spoken word poet, but she's also an artist! (**Link below[2]**). Saturnmoon for beautiful positivity and so much more.

A few more are Angelique, Ash, Phoenix, Lorelei, Enola, and Sir Von Doom, all of whom are so kind and supportive, and we connect through our poetry in such meaningful ways.

Thank you to Rocio B. Flores for letting me beta-read her debut poetry collection and for being so genuine, kind, and supportive. Her amazing poetry collection, *Untying You From Me*, comes out 11/18/2025! (**Link Below[3]**).

Thank you to Yaya Starchild for doing my first poetry exchange with me! I've found a kindred spirit in her poetry and personality. Her aptly named debut poetry collection, *Suncatcher Spirit*, just came out this past October! (**Link Below[4]**).

Thank you to my Stay community: Sienna, Melanie, Shannon, Jackie, Cristy, and Ritten Rhapsody. I never expected to make so many friends in Stayville, and I'm so happy I have! All absolute sweethearts!

Another seemingly random thank you to Stray Kids because I love writing (and I was definitely formatting) while listening to their music (on a damn loop)! Sometimes I get way too shy thinking about releasing my poetry, and I'm terrified of mean criticism. But they are such an inspiration through their words, music, and entire journey—it encourages me to keep going.

"No matter what they say, no matter what we hear, no matter what kind of evaluation we get… so what?"—Han Jisung

Fun Links!

1. **Sienna's Original Stickers:** https://www.etsy.com/shop/StaySticker Shop
2. **Helen's Art:** https://artisthelenleigh.yourwebsitespace.com/
3. **Rocio's Poetry:** *Untying You From Me:* https://a.co/d/4hft4kB
4. **Yaya's Poetry:** *Suncatcher Spirit:* https://pastelpoetics.com/product.html?id=1

Resources – Nonprofits

*Note: These are not comprehensive lists; there are plenty more resources and nonprofits out there; these are just a few to be (hopefully) helpful.

Resource List:

- **988 Suicide & Crisis Lifeline:** https://988lifeline.org/
- **American Association on Health & Disability (AAHD):** https://linktr.ee/aahealthdisability
- **Child Help:** (National Child Abuse Hotline): https://www.childhelp.org/hotline/
- **Feeding America:** (local food bank finder): https://www.feedingamerica.org/find-your-local-foodbank
- **Immigrant Defense Project:** https://www.immigrantdefenseproject.org/
- **National Domestic Violence Hotline:** https://www.thehotline.org/
- **RAINN'S National Sexual Assault Hotline:** https://rainn.org/help-and-healing/hotline/
- **The Trevor Project:** (Crisis Care for LGBTQ+ young people): https://www.thetrevorproject.org/crisis-services/
- **Trans Lifeline:** https://translifeline.org/

Nonprofits to Support:

- **Alexandra House:** (Working to end domestic and sexual violence): https://www.alexandrahouse.org/
- **Dahnoun Mutual Aid:** (Direct Support for Families in Gaza): https://chuffed.org/project/115245-dahnoun-mutual-aid
- **Feeding America:** (Uniting communities to end hunger): https://www.feedingamerica.org/
- **International Rescue Committee:** (Responds to the world's worst humanitarian crises): https://www.rescue.org/
- **The Arc:** (Support the fight for disability rights): https://thearc.org/
- **WANGO:** World Association of Non-Governmental Organizations: (Connecting & Serving NGOs Beyond Borders): https://www.wango.org/

Notes

SPELLING STRAWBERRY

1 **International Rescue Committee:** How to help Ukraine: https://www.rescue.org/article/how-can-i-help-ukraine

MY POETRY IS NECROMANCY

2 **International Rescue Committee:** https://www.rescue.org/

EVIL QUEENS

3 Passmore, J. (2025, January 2). *The underreporting and dismissal of sexual assault cases against women in the United States.* Ballard Brief. https://ballardbrief.byu.edu/issue-briefs/the-underreporting-and-dismissal-of-sexual-assault-cases-against-women-in-the-united-states

PRINCESS

4 **Domestic Violence Hotline:** https://www.thehotline.org/

BEASTLY BEAUTIFUL

5 Miralrío, A. (2022, July 30). *How Do Beauty Standards Affect Mental Health?.* https://www.amitydetroitcounseling.com/. https://www.amitydetroitcounseling.com/blog/what-is-beauty-culture-and-how-does-it-impact-mental-health

TAKE BACK THE NIGHT

6 **RAINN'S National Sexual Assault Hotline:** https://rainn.org/help-and-healing/hotlin e/

TRICKLE, RECYCLE, ABUSE

7 Button, A. (2023, July 14). *Understanding the Importance of Water Conservation - What Can I Do.* https://earth.org/. https://earth.org/understanding-the-importance-of-water-conservation/

8 Picchi, A. (2020, December 17). *50 years of tax cuts for the rich failed to trickle down, economics study says.* www.cbsnews.com. https://www.cbsnews.com/news/tax-cuts-rich-50-years-no-trickle-down/

About the Author

Kristen Jewel is an anti-fascist, feminist, spoken word poet and fiction writer (novel incoming). This is her second poetry collection, both released in 2025. On the side, she's a freelance editor and beta reader on Fiverr and a craft maker/seller on Etsy. She lives with her boyfriend, David, and their two pets, Khaleesi (cat) and Grogu (tortoise). She is a self-proclaimed enthusiastic Stay, loves pastels, and thinks pickleball just might be a conspiracy theory.

You can connect with me on:

- https://www.kristenjewel-writing.com
- https://linktr.ee/KristenJewel
- https://www.instagram.com/kristenjewel_writing
- https://www.threads.com/@kristenjewel_writing
- https://www.tiktok.com/@kristenjewel_writing
- https://www.youtube.com/@kristenjewel143
- https://www.fiverr.com/s/ljKEWog
- https://stayvilla.etsy.com

Also by Kristen Jewel

❦

More Than Half-Drowning is Kristen Jewel's debut poetry collection, released 1/1/2025.

More Than Half-Drowning

https://a.co/d/5C4sSas

"The human body contains 60% water, but it's grief I'm more than half-drowning in. How is that possible?"

More Than Half-Drowning is a poetry collection exploring the themes of sadness, anger, love, and low self-esteem. Divided into these four parts, the book delves into feeling emotions so strongly that it feels like you're physically drowning in them.

The feelings poetically captured in this book are relatable to anyone who has gone through a hard time. The author wrote this collection to share her experiences and ability to process these feelings—or even inability. She wrote this in the hope that anyone who feels similarly knows they are not alone. Anyone can feel like they are *More Than Half-Drowning*.